Fashioning the Feminine

Fashioning the Feminine

REPRESENTATION AND WOMEN'S
FASHION FROM THE FIN DE SIECLE
TO THE PRESENT

Cheryl Buckley and Hilary Fawcett

I.B. Tauris *Publishers*
LONDON • NEW YORK

Published in 2002 by I.B.Tauris & Co Ltd
6 Salem Road, London W2 4BU
175 Fifth Avenue, New York NY 10010
www.ibtauris.com

In the United States and Canada distributed by St. Martin's Press
175 Fifth Avenue, New York NY 10010

ISBN   1 86064 506 2 (PB)

A full CIP record for this book is available from the British Library
A full CIP record for this book is available from the Library of Congress

Library of Congress catalog card: available

Typeset in Bodoni by Dexter Haven Associates, London
Printed and bound in Great Britain by MPG Books Ltd. Bodmin, Cornwall

Contents

For our children:

Leo, Kate, Tom and Anna

Acknowledgements

We would like to thank all the people and organisations who have helped with the preparation of this book. Almost everyone that we have encountered in libraries, museums, local authorities and private companies have given their practical help without question. There are several women who gave us their time talking about their lives and recounting the clothes that they bought, made and wore; without their stories we could not have attempted to go beyond the abstract to examine the specific. There are a number of colleagues and friends whose involvement has been critical in talking over ideas, commenting on the draft, or just giving us support or space as and when we needed it. Several of these are our colleagues in the School of Humanities at the University of Northumbria, others are old friends, who include Rosie Betterton, Allan Cassidy, Ysanne Holt, Pat Kirkham, Kelly Lumley, Lynne Walker and Rosie White.

List of Illustrations

---

* It has proved impossible to identify copyright ownership of this, despite all reasonable
efforts. The authors would be pleased to hear from anyone who could help with this.

1 Introduction
Fashioning the Feminine: Fashion, Gender and Representation

This book has taken rather longer to write than we anticipated. It has been worked on intensely and it has been set aside, depending on the time and space that we have or have not found. It has been slowed down by the usual things in women's lives: busy jobs, dealing with young children and grown-up ones, and coping with illness. Our original aims, written at the beginning of the last decade, seem rather grand now at the start of a new millennium. We planned a broad survey of fashion in Britain between 1890 and 1999, highlighting the relationships between fashion, gender and representation. This ambition came out of our joint perception that fashion was only occasionally addressed comprehensively and rigorously in academic writing. Things have inevitably moved on, and the length of the book's genesis has worked to our advantage. Whereas ten, even five years ago, the books that dealt with fashion and gender in a historical context were few and far between, now many more exist. Not only are there a number of insightful accounts of its histories and meanings, fashion has now become more respected as a subject for study and research. In today's academic world, trivialising the everyday and the popular is intellectually insupportable, as studies in women's history, design history and material culture, and popular culture have given legitimacy to the study of fashion, whereas theoretical debates informed by post-structuralism, Marxism, post-modernism and feminism have helped to shape its intellectual development.

Undoubtedly we are the beneficiaries of these changes, and as a consequence we have sharpened the focus of our research and writing as the broad sweep appeared a less desirable strategy. Instead we have approached the history of twentieth-century fashion in Britain through a number of case studies which have aimed to 'locate' fashion during a specific 'time', between 1890 and 1990, and in a particular 'place', Britain. In adopting this approach, we are responding to the plethora of theories emerging from numerous disciplines, including cultural geography, material and cultural studies and gender studies, which have addressed important questions regarding history, representation, meaning, space and identity. Our aim has been to identify a number of 'historical moments' in Britain in the twentieth century, so as to explore the shifting meanings of fashion, particularly in relation to gender and representation. If we have had a 'guiding light' in this process, it has been without doubt feminism. Feminism has formed the backbone to our intellectual development, providing both method and motivation for our research. Its richness and diversity has engaged, persuaded and occasionally infuriated us. At the same time it has been at the core of our 15 year-old friendship and close working relationship, and it has 'enabled' us to see the political significance of our personal experiences. Working in a large new university, we have witnessed enormous changes which have both curtailed and expanded our opportunities. It is this context which has played a critical role in determining the direction and purpose of our academic activities. During these years, we have taught and managed large numbers of practical design students, particularly those studying fashion, as well as humanities students studying the history of art, design and film, cultural history and women's studies. These students have influenced our intellectual interests as much as our peers as we responded to their unbounded enthusiasm for the history of fashion.

Inevitably we have each brought slightly different emphases to this work, which reflect our particular life experiences and which stem from the range of things that constitute our individual 'historical landscape'.[1] This is inevitably influenced by our family and personal backgrounds, the places in which we grew up, studied and now live, and the different academic traditions in which we have worked: Fine Art, English Literature, Art History and Design History. We are individually responsible for separate chapters, each of which build on long-standing research interests. Cheryl, who has contributed Chapters 3 and 4, has worked and published widely on issues of gender, modernism and design in Britain. Her particular interest has been in the inter-war period, and the work that she has done here in fashion builds on her considerable knowledge of this. Hilary has been working and has published on issues of representation and gender in the late nineteenth century, and more recently on contemporary material. The 15 years that we have worked together and our continued interest in feminism have made for similarities as well as differences in approach, which are complementary in the context of the book.

Each chapter is concerned with the multiplicity of cultural and social formations which go towards fashioning the feminine. In Chapter 2, we examine the relationship between femininity, the fashion industry and fashion imagery between 1890 and 1910, and in Chapter 5, which deals with aspects of contemporary fashion, gender and sexuality, we focus on fashion not just as clothing, but as representation, and in particular the 'ideals' of beauty that it helps to construct. Continuing some of these themes, but at the same time highlighting new ones, Chapters 3 and 4 investigate the discontinuities between fashionable ideals found in women's magazines, fashion photography and illustration, and women's experiences. This introductory chapter, which aims to consider a number of theoretical issues arising for those studying the history of fashion, was inevitably written last, thus allowing us to reflect upon the discursive destinations of our chapters, and enabling us to extrapolate from underlying trends and themes. Threading through all the chapters is an interest in the broader themes which shaped women's engagement with fashion and fashion iconographies, such as modernity and post-modernity, and identity, particularly in relation to gender, but also of class and region.

The history of fashion is a field of study which overlaps and impinges upon many others. Analysis of fashion, dress and clothing tends to crop up in a number of academic contexts: social and economic historians have used it as a barometer of social change and patterns of consumption; cultural theorists have interpreted it as a site of complex discursive practices; art historians have analysed dress as part of the 'visual' culture of a specific period; and design historians have viewed it as intrinsic to the processes of cultural production and consumption. In 1985, in the then ground-breaking *Adorned in Dreams: Fashion and Modernity*, Elizabeth Wilson, who ranks along with Angela McRobbie as one of the most significant contributors to the development of the subject in the last 15 years, described fashion as 'a kind of connective tissue of our cultural organism'.[2] For Wilson, dress acts as a metaphysical layer which mediates between the body, ostensibly natural, and the social and the cultural. In this work and subsequent texts, including the reader *Chic Thrills* (co-authored with Juliet Ash), Wilson attempts to interpret the meaning of the multiple layers that constitute fashion.[3] Informed by aspects of Marxism, post-modernism and feminism, Wilson consistently refuses the dominant interpretations of fashion: that it is a form of 'mindless' consumption, or the result of social envy; that it reveals psychological neuroses; or that it oppresses women. Instead she has aimed to highlight the subtleties, complexities and contradictions of meanings within fashion. The social, cultural and psychological significance of fashion has attracted the interest of a number of subsequent writers, including Valerie Steele, Christopher Breward, Jennifer Craik and Caroline Evans, all of whom have contributed to the richness of research, although all have come from different starting points.[4] In this book we draw on these approaches, but we hope that by foregrounding the issue of gender, these four in-depth case studies will add to the understanding of the meanings of twentieth-century fashion in Britain.

Britain is the place where our research is focused, and we are interested in fashion and the fashionable iconographies that were circulated and accessible in Britain at specific historical points. However, we are wary of a unified notion of 'Britishness' in relation to fashion, in that throughout the twentieth century the dominant language of fashion has been international, and more specifically, Western. Fashion, we argue, constructed and constituted identity, although a sense of national identity was effaced within dress by the very nature of fashion. Due to its symbiotic relationship to capitalism and the modern city, fashion crossed national boundaries, and if, as Wilson suggests 'Fashion is dress in which the key feature is rapid and continual changing of styles', then it has been and remains concentrated in the modern cities of London, New York, Milan, Tokyo and Paris.[5]

Wider access to fashion across social classes is, however, a characteristic of fashion in Britain in the twentieth century. As this study shows, the greater availability of fashion, and the knowledge required to dress fashionably, was enhanced by a number of factors. Firstly this resulted from new technologies in fabric production, garment construction and fashion promotion. These developed both in the home and at the factory, and were a consequence of the greater availability of the home sewing machine, but also they were due to the introduction of modern industrial methods. These included divisions of labour, which were organised to facilitate mass-production, the use of new machinery for sewing and cutting cloth, and latterly the increasingly sophisticated use of computer technology in the design, manufacturing and marketing of fashion. One direct outcome of this, affecting the fashion industry from the 1920s onwards, was the de-skilling of the tailoring trade, which had been dominated by men, and the introduction of cheaper semi-skilled female labour. Secondly, knowledge of the latest fashions and 'looks' both expanded and speeded up due to the phenomenal influence of magazines, film and television, theatre, music and pop videos. The rapid turnover of fashionable styles was remarked upon as early as the 1930s by retailers anxious to retain some control over an increasingly fickle consumer. As the century progressed, the consumer became better informed and less loyal to particular retailers. Finally, enormous changes in the retailing, marketing and promoting of fashion during the twentieth century have transformed accessibility to fashion. The 'cut and finish' of fashionable clothes may be hugely disparate and crucially dependent on income, lifestyles and patterns of consumption, but the 'look' of new fashionable styles is rapidly assimilated and adapted at all levels of the market. To be 'fashionable' is an option for most people living in Britain today.

For the first 60 years of the twentieth century, fashion was the embodiment of modernity, whereas since 1970 it revealed the conditions of late capitalism and exposed the contradictions of post-modernism. From the end of the nineteenth century, fashion was an important cultural site for the manifestation of the 'modern': it was urban and it constituted the type of visual spectacle which characterised the city.[6] The relentless cycles of stylistic change, the rapid technological advances, the expansion of markets, and the emergence of new forms of consumption – all features of modernity – were crucial factors in the development of fashion in twentieth-century Britain. The role of women in this was critical. Newly enfranchised with improved access to better types of work, especially from the Great War onwards, more women engaged with fashion than hitherto. Fashion provided a unique opportunity for women to experience modernity, and unusually it was a cultural activity which connected both the domestic and the public spheres. The consumption and display of fashion took place in the drawing room as well as at the theatre, and the whole paraphernalia of choosing, fitting, buying and dressing involved women in a number of sophisticated cultural choices which were in turn shaped by the broader social and cultural pre-occupations of the day.

Paradoxically, fashion as the epitome of 'the modern' challenged the rigid dogma of modernism. In its denial of universal values, it operated at a critical distance to the rigours of modernism. The ceaseless changes of fashion, which were intrinsic to it, undermined notions of 'good design' – a key element of modernism. In fact, integral to fashion and borne of its intimate relationship to capitalism was a form of built-in obsolescence which ensured an endless market ready to buy into the very latest and most modern styles. The relative nature of these styles represented a challenge to the hegemony of modernism, although at the same time a handful of fashion designers, such as Coco Chanel, sought to interpret modernism by simplifying fashion and seeking to establish strict codes of design.

The cultural relativity of fashion predisposed it to the challenge of post-modernism. Fashion since 1970 has provided an ideal cultural arena in which to observe the 'complexity and contradiction' which has characterised post-modernity. Indeed some of the strategies deployed early on in the work of pioneer post-modernists Denise Scott Brown and Robert Venturi in town planning, architecture and writing, which functioned to attack the formal orthodoxy of modernism, have been evident in fashion throughout the century.[7] Decoration and pattern, stylistic eclecticism and parody, and an enthusiasm for 'popular' culture can be found in the work of designers as diverse as Paul Poiret in the 1910s, Elsa Schiaparelli in the 1930s, and even Christian Dior in the 1940s and 1950s. Fashion's predilection for change leaves it susceptible and particularly responsive to the experience of post-modernity – to the dislocation, fragmentation and relativism that characterised Western societies and their cultures in the last quarter of the twentieth century. As this study will show, fashion, as a depository of cultural meanings and values, maps out the territories of modernity and post-modernity, and it marks the transition from one to the other most effectively.

Arguably, the social and cultural definitions of gender have been a key site for the delineation of the 'modern' and the 'post-modern'. Clear distinctions between the masculine and the feminine have been blurred in the twentieth century; indeed the meanings of both have been fiercely contested in the contexts of female suffrage, the huge structural changes to the economy which have undermined traditional male roles within the workplace and female roles at home, and more openness about sexuality and sexual orientation. Masculinity and femininity have been highly volatile and elusive concepts which have been negotiated and renegotiated within the context of modernity and post-modernity. Consider the experiences of young women in the 1930s with those today. Feminism has empowered women to make great strides over the last century, but although there have been many changes for the better in women's lives, there are still some surprising similarities. Social distinctions based on income and class, increasingly eroded in the 1930s due to women's access to better-paid work in manufacturing industry, were re-asserted with a vengeance at the end of the twentieth century, as women were concentrated in part-time, low-paid work in the service sector. The economic insecurities of late capitalism, an integral feature of post-modernity, have left a legacy of social exclusion and inequality in which gender roles represent a new set of battle lines.

Uniquely among cultural industries, fashion offers the opportunity for both public and private pleasures. It has been an arena in which women, in particular, have accrued power, although at the same time it has been a source of anxiety. To be 'fashionable' can be simultaneously delightful and cruel, attracting admiration as well as ridicule. The very process of being 'in fashion', ahead of the crowd, but part of it; of possessing a much admired pair of shoes or jacket; of knowing that the cut, fabric and colour of a specific outfit feels just right; and being able to put it all together to create a certain style; these are part of the pleasure and pride of fashion. For us (the authors) it has been a key element in our developing identities, and it has largely been a source of empowerment for both of us: as young women it has been a tool enabling us to represent our independence from family and home; as adult women it has allowed us to define our sense of 'self' in the changing contexts of work, sexuality and reproduction; and now, as we grow older, it is a key visual 'space' in which we negotiate who we are and who we might yet become. Born in the North of England after the Second World War, we have each witnessed the enormous shifts in the production and consumption of clothes, as increased affluence meant that shop-bought fashionable clothes were within the grasp of the lower-middle and working classes. From home-made clothes in childhood, 'mod' and 'ethnic' styles as teenagers, to the one-off luxury of designer garments as working women, our historical land-scapes can be charted through the clothes that we have bought and worn, and we can ponder retrospectively the significance of particular styles, looks and items of clothing at the different stages of our lives.

The ambiguities of fashion, and the ways in which it can transgress as well as reinforce dominant modes of representation, are the underlying themes of this book. Fashion defines gender, and renders it visible. But with-out question it is one of the most slippery of terms: it can be used in the sense of 'to fashion', 'fashionable', and to describe an area of design practice concerned with dress and clothing. Our interest in fashion cuts across these usages: we are concerned with fashion as design practice – and given our particular focus on the twentieth century, a period of modernity and post-modernity – we are also interested in the fashionable and the ways in which fashion has been subject to the vagaries of British capitalism over our period. But perhaps most important for this examination of gender and identity is the 'constructive' and 'constitutive' process of 'fashioning'.

Like the notion of 'becoming', 'fashioning' implies an endless process, rarely completed. Fashion can function then as a narrative of an individual life, but it is one usually without closure. Clothes are bought and worn as particular outfits, but these are then 're-constituted' with other clothes. The twentieth-century fashion business may still attempt to 'fix' a particular look through advertising and magazines, but alone of all aspects of design, fashion has the potential endlessly to deny this. In numerous major and minor ways, women can subvert these dominant representations of the 'fashionable', more so since 1900 as fashion information has become more available. Inevitably there have been and remain real constraints to this. Dominant fashionable ideals are projected in magazines, in the cinema and on television, and these are powerful and effective persuaders. An ever-expanding market means that girls as young as eight years old can readily copy the styles and looks of their pop idols, Shania Twain or 'Posh' Spice, Victoria Adams. At the close of the century, there is not one look, but several, and these can be combined in ways which undercut dominant, 'preferred' meanings or readings. The extent to which these are genuinely empowering in the context of post-modern culture is, however, highly questionable.

As this book demonstrates, definitions of femininity have fragmented in the twentieth century, and it is no longer possible to write of them as a single unified concept. The boundaries of gender identities have blurred as female roles have changed beyond recognition from those of our grandmothers and their mothers. As the meanings of femininity have been mediated by class, race, age, national identity and sexuality, we increasingly recognise that gender identities are not fixed but always in the process of making. Informed by psychoanalysis, post-modernism and especially feminism, writers such as

Rosi Braidotti and Judith Butler attempt to describe and assess the implications of the transitory nature of 'gendered identity'. Braidotti talks of women as 'nomadic subjects', whereas Butler describes gender as 'performative'.[8] Like many contemporary feminists, Braidotti is concerned to recognise the differences between women and the 'politics of their location', so as not to reassert a form of biological essentialism. A 'politics of location' aims to take account of 'the interconnectedness between identity, subjectivity, and power. The self being a sort of network of interrelated points...'[9] Her 'nomadic consciousness', which is an essential element in her attempt to articulate a subversive notion of femininity, is a mechanism to enable women to dis-identify with what she sees as the paralysing structures of patriarchy (although she writes specifically about philosophy, her ideas are pertinent to other academic subjects). Using a term from Foucault, she describes the nomadic consciousness as a 'countermemory', which has the capacity 'to enact a rebellion of subjugated knowledges'.[10] Like a number of other feminist writers, such as bell hooks in her book *Yearning*, Sally Alexander in her essay 'Becoming a Woman', and Carolyn Steadman in 'Landscape of a Good Woman', she is concerned to 'situate' femininity, to ground it in time and place so as to move beyond the abstract and the universal in the hope that it might represent the personal and the particular of 'women's lived experiences'.[11]

Fashion history does not constitute a 'subjugated knowledge', although it is certainly the case that, except in a handful of cases, the detailed relationships between women and fashion have been seriously overlooked. The historiography of fashion is dominated by famous designer names, or those who have claimed genius or have been so described. Such an approach is exacerbated by an industry which thrives on 'stars', whether they be larger-than-life *auteur* designers or well-known film and pop-star consumers. The styles of the rich and powerful have figured prominently in many accounts of fashion in the twentieth century, as have the activities of innovative retailers, avant-garde photographers, and creative promoters. Until the last 20 years or so, fashion history had not been particularly interested in the intimacies of women's relationships with fashion, although writers including Angela Partington and Angela McRobbie have produced influential essays and books which make important contributions to this.[12] Arguably, if there is a subjugated knowledge of fashion, it is women's specific experiences of it. This type of 'knowledge of fashion' should, of necessity, be 'closely connected to one's place of enunciation, that is, where one is actually speaking from'.[13] In such a context, fashion takes on huge significance for women if, as Braidotti has argued, the primary site from which women speak is the body, which is 'an interface, a threshold, a field of intersecting forces where multiple codes are inscribed'.[14] Fashion effectively functions as the primary language in which the majority of women can converse in a variety of ways;

its codes are visual, and consciously and unconsciously these enunciate aspects of the social and the cultural self in both public and private arenas.

Due to this intimacy with the body, fashion is a critical tool for representing femininity. It is highly effective in endlessly constituting but never fixing identities, and it is performative, in that it ceaselessly rehearses and enacts the 'lines' of femininity. In this respect it can be a mechanism of social control and manipulation, but also, as we will see in a number of the case studies in this book, it has the potential for transgression and disruption. Historically it is possible to see that fashion sometimes crosses the boundaries of what is acceptable, to become genuinely subversive. To be glamorous in the 1930s was a parody of accepted feminine styles, whereas the highly casual and 'masculinised' clothes adapted by munition and factory workers during the First World War undercut rigid class and gender identities. At the same time it can function normatively by attempting to 'fix' feminine identities in ways which merely support the status quo. Images in *Vogue* magazine during the First World War deployed fashion and particular female iconography to evoke class and racial purity through an idealised form of femininity. More recently, images in a magazine such as *More* can be seen to consolidate dominant femininities in contemporary culture.

This book is based on two key assumptions: one, that historically fashion has functioned in complex and interesting ways to construct feminine identities; and two, that these ways have yet to be fully explored. Our aim has been to offer a number of insights into this process, rather than to come to any final conclusions. The four case studies on which the book is based are obviously 'snapshots' of relatively short historical periods, and, like photographs, although they may resemble reality we know that in fact they give us only part of the picture. Indeed, to depict the full historical picture appears utopian, and perhaps misguided. Like femininity, histories are rarely 'complete'. In fact it seems to us that reinterpreting and reshaping history is one of its disciplinary attractions, and as new research is under-taken and fresh perspectives come into view, the challenge for historians is to add new ways of seeing.

In Chapter 2, which deals with fashion and femininity between 1890 and 1910, we argue that in a number of ways the fashionable ideal of the period pre-empted modernity, and that the commodification of femininity was a key element in the emergence of modernity. New ways of making clothes and the subsequent wider availability of fashionable styles have already been acknowledged as critical to this process, but perhaps just as essential were the techniques and devices which went into 'constructing' the ideal consumer of fashion. These include the expansion of fashion retailing, particularly within the department store; the opening of hairdressing salons and the establishment of beauty consultancies; and the popularisation of cosmetics.

All of these were promoted in the plethora of women's magazines which emerged at the end of the nineteenth and beginning of the twentieth centuries through an advertising industry which, by deploying the latest illustrative and photographic processes in an increasingly sophisticated manner, aimed to widen the fashion market by drawing the middle classes into the privileged world of high fashion.

As well-established houses such as Redfern and Creed were joined in the 1890s and 1900s by newcomers Lucile and Reville and Rossiter, *haute couturiers* in Britain began to compete with the dominant French houses Paquin, Callot-Soeurs and Worth. The close relationship between the English upper classes and *haute couture* was challenged by the popularity of a number of independent, though mainly married, women in the 1900s, some of whom were actresses. The 'stars' of their day, these women were dressed for their theatrical performances as well as for their glamorous social lives by couturiers such as Lucile, who, in fact, adopted theatrical devices for her fashion shows. Glamour, eroticism and spectacle were essential elements of her designs, which suggested in dress the world of romance which her sister Elinor Glyn described in her novels. Sexual licence and social independence, within certain patriarchal constraints, accompanied the lifestyles of those who wore such designs, and women such as Lily Langtry and Daisy Warwick exercised an autonomy in their sexual conduct which was a world apart from women outside their specific social milieu. Fashion designers responded to this sexually mature femininity, and although the period was characterised by anxieties about the nature of female sexuality, these were contained by patriarchy, as these glamorous older women conducted their affairs strictly within the confines of their marriages. Typically more statuesque, curvaceous and weighty, this 'ideal' represented the contradictory forces operating at the time with regard to femininity. In some ways highly incongruous in an era of modernity, this highly decorative, sumptuous image nevertheless demonstrates how fashion and its associated ephemera mediated the contradictions inherent in women's shifting social, political and sexual identities at the time.

In identifying the First World War as 'the breakdown of the (western) civilisation of the nineteenth century', Eric Hobsbawn reinforces a trend evident in the work of a number of historians by viewing the war as the point at which the twentieth century began.[15] In fact the First World War speeded up a period of transformation which was evident by the end of the nineteenth century, and which saw social and economic change precipitated by the increasingly effective labour and feminist movements, and by strong economic competition from powerful trading rivals. Discussing the significance of visual images in representing these transformations, Deborah Cherry and Jane Beckett argue that these 'did particular ideological work in the representation of masculinity, femininity, class and race'.[16] Chapter 3 considers the ways in which visual images, particularly those produced in fashion and its related media, mediated those changes for women. To sustain the expanding clothing industry, and supported by cheaper women's magazines such as *Home Chat*, women were targeted as consumers of fashion as never before. The fashionable female body was not, however, merely a passive surface on which the dominant feminine ideal could be mapped out. Due to the profound experience of war and war work, many more women were empowered to take a hand in their aesthetic and cultural identities as well as their social ones. The female body during wartime literally became a battle site, as women's magazines, fashion designers and photographers attempted to come to terms with the enormous social, cultural and economic changes wrought by the impact of war. Openly wearing masculinised forms of dress, as well as more informal, casual clothes which equipped them for work previously done by men outside the home, women's appearance on the streets of British towns and cities was an affront to patriarchy. Dressing fashionably, eating out alone, and managing significantly increased wages represented a challenge to the patriarchal order which was noted by social commentators and newspaper editors alike.

Fashion, however, was inherently modern, and it offered a transformative space in which women could attempt to mark out their personal sense of modernity, one which was as much to do with the private body as with the public world. It remained, however, a crucially significant 'feminine' space, and this was underscored in lower-middle-class magazines such as *Home Chat* and in the upmarket *Vogue*. Addressing a wider audience, *Home Chat* attempted to track its readers' interests, and in doing so reflected and encouraged women's changing roles alongside a consistent concern for the traditional accoutrements of femininity, including fashion. Largely immune to the war, except in a superficial way, *Vogue*, although highly modern in style and design, maintained a commitment to a very specific form of class and gender identity which attempted to ignore the social transformations produced by wartime. Fashionable women were typically child-like in appearance, passively representing a racially pure feminine 'ideal' at a time when the British empire was threatened by Germany and its colonies. Paradoxically, the fashionable styles of dress, with their linear, simplified cut, bold colour and pattern – which were illustrated in both *Home Chat* and *Vogue*, and were influenced by the pre-war couturier Paul Poiret – epitomised a feeling for modernity clearly at odds with the values of the established, patriarchal order which had led Britain into war. Empowered by their wartime experiences, some women were able to respond to this feeling for modernity and to use the language of fashion to represent this.

Increasingly intolerant of their elders, fashion became a powerful tool in challenging patriarchy (albeit sometimes unconsciously) for some women in the inter-war years. As we argue in Chapter 4, it both symbolised the changes which women had experienced and provided an exciting visual medium in which women could begin to represent themselves as feminine at a time when gender identity was being renegotiated. Single women with a degree of disposable income, including some from the working class as well as the middle class, were the primary market for the latest fashionable styles, although better-off married women made ideal consumers as a result of the new selling techniques of credit and mail order deployed by large department stores.

Fashion offered more women than previously the possibility of wearing smart clothes which bore the stylistic imprint of *haute couture*, even if they were the product of home dressmaking, or the improved mass-production processes found in the new clothing factories emerging in the 1930s. Indeed women's complex relationship to fashion was conditioned by modernity, and at the same time was a sign of it. Women were consumers of the fashionable styles available in the new multiple stores, and illustrated in women's and film magazines; they were producers of clothes at home or in the factory; and they were saleswomen and buyers of fashion in the large department stores.

The greater availability of information about fashion, particularly in women's magazines but increasingly through Hollywood cinema and film magazines, provided women with the means to follow fashion as never before. Glamour, Hollywood-style, gave women a visual vocabulary based on the notion that looks were made rather than born. Beauty and style could be seen to come in many guises, and some of these were deliberately provocative in relation to gender. The knowledgeable young consumer of fashion could emulate the arch femininity of Jean Harlow, the girl-next-door looks of Jean Arthur or, conversely, interpret the casual masculinity of Katherine Hepburn or the gender ambiguities with which both Greta Garbo and Marlene Dietrich toyed in their respective ways. Becoming a woman was exposed as a role to be played, and the notion that femininity was somehow fixed, an essential element of being born female, was revealed as a fiction. Fashion was in many ways a metaphor for the social, political and cultural changes shaping women's lives and, along with many other experiences, it undermined patri- archal values. Only a privileged few fitted the stereotype of 'gay young thing', however, it is clear through the analysis of fashion illustrations, photographs and particular fashionable looks that many women were influenced, sometimes in small ways, by the notion that different femininities could be constructed. Fashion provided an arena in which women could imagine them- selves differently and, even if only for short periods of their lives, this was highly significant because of its intimacy with the female body.

An intense focus on sexuality has characterised the relationship between fashion and the female body since the 1960s. By looking at the experience of young women as consumers of fashion in Newcastle-upon-Tyne in 1999, Chapter 5 explores the complex ways in which femininity, feminism and sexual identity coalesce in the marketplace for contemporary fashion and visual identities, particularly as seen in contemporary women's magazines. Looking back over the last 15 years – a period of de-industrialisation in Northeast England, with attempted renewal, but at a price – sexual identity has been a highly contentious arena for both men and women. At the same time, sustained attacks on second-wave feminism, the emergence of post-feminism, and a general shift to the political right, has left a vacuum in which female sexuality is defined and redefined in ways which are highly problematic. The challenging visual identities which emerged for women in the 1970s in the context of punk fashion and imagery have been replaced by essentially patriarchal definitions of female sexuality best summed up by the image of pop icon Madonna. Hailed as a liberator of women by vociferous academic and popular writers, Madonna has been responsible for articulating female desire as active, but by drawing on a visual language that is essentially patriarchal. Theoretical inertia and accusations of puritanism have rendered feminist opposition largely ineffective, and left today's young women without a political voice. As this study shows, Newcastle's two principal party areas, the Bigg Market and the Quayside, are permeated with a masculinised drinking culture in which young women attempt to participate as men's equals. This strategy essentially re-works the 'equal but different' thinking of some inter-war feminists, as gender difference is aggressively marked out by dress codes which mimic a glittery, glamorous 'babe' ideal. In an area in which job prospects and life opportunities are limited, this highly eroticised femininity can be read as a representation of powerlessness rather than power. In this context, fashion operates to render women's powerlessness visible, rather than to provide a new language for female empowerment.

Writing in 1976 in his revised edition of *On Human Finery*, Quentin Bell speculated on whether 'fashion is on its way out?' Bell conceived of fashion primarily as a vehicle for the maintenance of status, yet 25 years later we can see that it is arguably more pervasive than at any other time, and in the twentieth century in particular it has functioned in increasingly subtle and complex ways. It has been a key cultural site in which the feminine has been constituted; it has provided women with a visual language which has mainly enriched their everyday lives; and, importantly for feminists, it has exposed the body as a socio-cultural artefact rather than a biological essence. In this book we show how fashion can be transgressive and disruptive of dominant representational codes, yet at the same time reinforcing them, and operate as a device which placates women within patriarchy. Fashion's inherent instability within the contexts of modernity, post-modernity and shifting gender relations in twentieth-century Britain is its chief disciplinary appeal both at the personal and academic levels. From a personal perspective, it has provided a means of making visible our changing sense of identity at the different stages of our lives, whereas on the academic front, as the four case studies show, it is the key cultural site for fashioning the feminine.

NOTES ON CHAPTER 1

1   A term used by Carolyn Steadman in her essay 'Landscape For a Good Woman', published in Liz Heron (ed.), *Truth, Dare or Promise: Girls Growing Up in the 50s* (London, Virago, 1985), pp.103–26.
2   Elizabeth Wilson, *Adorned in Dreams: Fashion and Modernity* (London, Virago, 1985), p.12. Angela McRobbie has written extensively on fashion. Recent work includes *British Fashion Design: Rag Trade or Image Industry?* (London, Routledge, 1998).
3   Juliet Ash and Elizabeth Wilson (eds), *Chic Thrills: A Fashion Reader* (London, Pandora, 1992).
4   Valerie Steele, *Fashion and Eroticism: Ideals of Feminine Beauty from the Victorian to the Jazz Age* (Oxford, Oxford University Press, 1985); Christopher Breward, *The Culture of Fashion: A New History of Fashionable Dress* (Manchester, Manchester University Press, 1995); Caroline Evans and Minna Thornton, *Women and Fashion: A New Look* (London, Quartet Books, 1989); Jennifer Craik, *The Face of Fashion: Cultural Studies in Fashion* (London, Routledge, 1994).
5   Wilson, *Adorned in Dreams*, p.3.
6   Wilson discusses these ideas in full.
7   Denise Scott Brown and Robert Venturi, *Complexity and Contradiction in Architecture* (New York, Museum of Modern Art, 1966); *Learning From Las Vegas* (London, MIT Press, 1972).
8   Rosi Braidotti, *Nomadic Subjects: Embodiment and Sexual Difference in Contemporary Feminist Theory* (New York, Columbia University Press, 1994); Judith Butler, *Gender Trouble: Feminism and the Subversion of Identity* (London, Routledge, 1990).
9   Braidotti, *Nomadic Subjects*, p.31.
10   Ibid., p.25.
11   bell hooks, *Yearning: Race, Gender and Cultural Politics* (London, Turnaround, 1991); Sally Alexander, *Becoming a Woman and Other Essays in 19th and 20th Century Feminist History* (London, Virago, 1994); Caroline Steadman, 'Landscape of a Good Woman'.
12   See, for example, Angela McRobbie, *Zoot Suits and Second-Hand Dresses: An Anthology of Fashion and Music* (London, Macmillan, 1989); Angela Partington, 'Popular Fashion and Working-class Affluence', in Ash and Wilson (eds), *Chic Thrills*.

13   Braidotti, *Nomadic Subjects*, p.237.

14   Ibid., p.238.

15   Eric Hobsbawn, *The Age of Extremes: The Short Twentieth Century 1914–1991* (London, Michael Joseph, 1994), p.6.

16   Jane Beckett and Deborah Cherry, *The Edwardian Era* (London, Phaidon, 1987), p.14.

2 Fashion, Sexuality and Representation at the *Fin de Siècle*

Would you like to sin
with Elinor Glyn
On a tiger skin?

This chapter examines the relationship between femininity, fashion and fashion imageries in Britain between 1890 and 1910. The period has been described as a 'battlefield of representation',[1] marked as it is on one side by an acceleration in the progress of feminism and its attendant imageries, and on the other by representations of extravagant femininity in the highly decorative and seductive arena of high fashion. The monumentality of the Edwardian beauty, resplendent in the sumptuous clothing of the day, conveyed an extraordinary visual power. There is a need to understand the factors involved in the construction of such an image, which in its imposing confidence might be considered paradoxical in the light of the fraught nature of the social, political and cultural status of women at the *fin de siècle*.

Photographs of Edwardian beauties dressed in the elaborate designs of Worth, Lucile or Callot Seors contain a certain self-parodying glamour, a hyper-femininity similar to that found in the exaggerated artifice of male transvestitism. Fashionable clothing in this period was characterised by excess, by the use of luxurious and sensual fabrics heavily trimmed in lace, and exquisite detail. Hats were large and sweeping, decorated with feathers and flowers. Luxuriant hair was rolled and padded with horsehair in order to create height and volume, and the increasing use of cosmetics contributed to the highly stylised and artificial look (Figure 2.1). Images of fashionable women found in newspapers, magazines, on postcards and billboards were overtly fetishised but retained an incontrovertible dimension of sumptuous female authority that defies a crudely reductivist explanation based on class and gender stereotyping.

This chapter attempts to re-evaluate the period in relation to women and fashion, and the way in which it pre-empts modernity. Much writing on the period has been dominated by debates concerning the issues of corseting and tight lacing and the role of the oppositional dress reform movement in countering what was considered to be restrictive and unhealthy dress for women. Although these issues are of considerable significance, this chapter will concentrate on other aspects of the subject. Its focus is on fashionable clothing, but also on the fashionable ideal of beauty, with particular reference to its representation and promotion in the printed media and wider visual culture. It looks at high fashion in a metropolitan arena, and at the consumers who engaged in this expanding and changing culture.

Outside the privileged milieu of the wealthy socialite, fashion at this time was engaging an ever wider public, and industrial developments – beginning with the sewing machine, followed by blind-stitching machines, and later pressing machines and steam irons[2] – allowed for the mass-production of certain garment types, thus involving markets directly and

more rapidly in the fashion process. New emphasis was placed on areas such as cosmetics and hairdressing, with salons and consultancies opening in major cities and advertising in the expanding magazine industry playing an increasingly important role in the marketing of beauty-orientated products. High fashion, through illustrations in magazines and the increasing photo-graphic presence of the rich and famous 'a la mode' across the media – which increased in the early 1900s due to developments in photographic technique[3] – created a wider public awareness of stylistic mores and encouraged the development of a culture of aspiration for those women excluded from the privileged world of the upper classes. The expansion and proliferation of department stores, especially in London, allowed middle-class access to a version of this world of luxury and consumption, and the development of new markets, such as perfume produced by couturiers, at this time enabled the middle-class consumer to be associated with the exclusive rites of high fashion. This represents not only a significant change in the fashion industry itself but also the first real thrust in the process of the commodification of femininity as we have become accustomed to understand it.

Figure 2.1: Advertisement for the Marvel Fringe. *Lady's Pictorial*, 14 December 1895.

London was the centre of new and exciting developments in the retailing of fashion, and offered a bustling and energetic background to the new rituals of consumption for women. Erika Diane Rappaport, in discussing consumption in London's West End in the period, describes the spectacle of the window displays of Selfridges in Oxford Street, which were lit up at night to attract the attention of theatre-goers and others seeking an evening's recreation in the city.[4] Department stores offered middle-class women – through their window displays, advertisements and the structure of the shops themselves – a version of the world represented on the society pages of magazines. Rappaport refers to the romanticisation of urban space which this new culture of consumption brought to the West End of London, an area previously associated with 'prostitution, gambling and other illicit activities'.[5] The themes of glamour and romance were all-pervasive in the period, and ranged across the developing cultures of consumption for women.

The issue of class was central to the identity of fashion markets. High fashion was the principal source of stylistic innovation, and influenced the design of clothing from department store replicas to home dressmaking patterns. High fashion, in the form of *couture*, was essentially metropolitan, with many of those engaged in it being part of the London season. Although there was this broadening of markets at the turn of the century, it was only the very rich who engaged directly with *haute couture* at its source in the expanding milieu of the fashion house. This is a period marked by the rise of the *nouveau riche*, that group of financiers and entrepreneurs from a variety of national backgrounds, such as the Courtaulds, the Tennants and the de Rothschilds who socialised with the aristocracy and who played a significant role in the formation of popular taste in the period.

In the 1890s, Paris was pivotal to the process of fashion, and the fashion houses of Worth and Paquin were of particular importance. The concept of *haute couture*, as initiated by Worth, was still relatively new, and had been traditionally identified with the status and wealth of European royalty and aristocracy. The process of buying these clothes was one approached with discretion. The customer would go to the salon and 'here with her vendeuse, one of the couturier's team of sales women with whom she always dealt and who knew all her personal and financial secrets, she would choose her wardrobe for the next six months'.[6] When Madam Isadore Paquin eventually opened a salon in Dover Street in London for her British clients in 1913, she was to join a group of French couturiers, including Worth, who had established premises there in the early 1900s and who had expanded their clientele amongst the wealthy middle class.

By the late nineteenth century, British designers were beginning to make inroads into particular aspects of the upper part of the market. British tailoring firms Charles Creed and Redfern both had salons in Conduit Street, off Oxford Street, from the late 1880s, and were instrumental in the development of the 'tailor-made', a form of tailored suiting for women that became popular as day wear and which was seen as characteristically British in its allusions to country sports and the men's tailoring industry of Saville Row. Also by the 1900s, designers such as Lucile, originally Mrs James Wallace, had established themselves in London, catering for the more glamorous side of the fashion market, previously identified with Paris. Lucile is of significance in this study in the context of the construction of a particular femininity in the period. The glamour and ostentation which characterised her designs was also to be found in many London interiors of the period such as those designed for Leopold de Rothschild and and the Bass family.[7] The fact that so many of the new rich in Britain had come from other parts of Europe brought interesting and different influences to play in the construction of popular taste, and the developing British fashion industry was responsive to this new exoticism.

Fashion and interiors were not the only areas in which there was a new aesthetic of display and spectacle. The ideal female beauty of the day was of a type that would have been considered vulgar to earlier Victorians, for whom good breeding, daintiness and delicacy were defining attributes. Corn-fed American socialites such as Jennie Jerome, later Lady Randolph Churchill, who had married into the British establishment in the 1870s and 1880s, were influential in the development of a new and more robustly seductive female ideal. Statuesque and exotically dark, due in part to her native American ancestry, Lady Churchill combined a frank and open manner with an eager sensuality. Her contemporary Lily Langtry, a great favourite of the Prince of Wales, was another beauty whose powerful looks contributed to a defining fashionable femininity in the later part of the century. Her humble origins in the Channel Islands were no impediment to her enormous social success, and her later success in the theatre. Those who, like Langtry, combined theatrical careers with the role of society beauty had substantial iconic power in this period.

The powerful physicality that characterised fashionable female imagery was also influenced by the contemporary artistic preference for classicism. Painters attached to this style, such as Alfred Lord Leighton and Lawrence Alma Tadema, were enormously popular with a broad audience, as their work was shown in the ever-increasing number of municipal art galleries opening across Britain. The classical beauties who peopled their paintings were handsome young women with strong and regular profiles and ample figures. The Edwardian female ideal also, however, owed something to the female imagery of Pre-Raphaelite painters of the 1850s and 1860s, in particular the later paintings of Dante Gabriel Rossetti. These works, when first painted, had appealed to an exclusive artistic elite, but by the late century elements of the imagery were incorporated into popular iconography. Griselda Pollock has discussed Rossetti's later paintings, and their significance in relation to 'a new regime of representation of woman on the axis of bourgeois realism and erotic fantasy'.[8] This material represented a new glamour, a construction of a female identity created within a particular locus of class within the medium of painting at a point immediately before the camera began to take precedence in the articulation of female representation. Pollock states of these paintings: 'At a manifest level they are specifically about sexuality, attempting to stabilise positions of masculinity and femininity through the language/hierarchies of romantic love'.[9] It is this conjunction of sensuality and romantic love that was to remain a recurring theme in the cultural production of femininity through the late nineteenth into the early twentieth century. The strong jaw and almost masculine bone structure of Pre-Raphaelite 'stunners' in works such as Rossetti's 'Bocca Bocciata' is ameliorated in its harshness by reddened bee-stung lips and whitened skin, which flatten the image and give the impression of the subject wearing makeup, an unacceptable practice for respectable women of the period, but which by the 1890s had become commonplace in the toilette of the fashionable middle class and aristocracy. Pollock discusses the processes of fetishisation at play in these representations, and their significance in the development of the female iconographies of modernity: 'the image is played across by conflicting possibilities of pleasure, fear and loss'.[10] As 'face objects' they prefigured Hollywood cinema, and they also connected more immediately with the qualities of the promotional images attached to fashionable beauty and the theatre in the late nineteenth century, which were shared by female stars of stage and society alike.

There was a very strong link between the theatre and high fashion in this period. Only a few decades before, the theatrical profession had been of a very low status, but with an increase in good writing for the stage and in the public desire for entertainment by the late 1890s there were 38 theatres in London and a great number of music halls.[11] The theatre and music hall became central to the construction of ideals of female beauty, and postcards and other ephemera attached to the entertainment industry were part of an expanding iconography operating around a newly articulated concept of glamour that prefigured the Hollywood star system. The notion of glamour, of 'made-upness',[12] found in later Rossetti paintings, and which is attached to the growing commodification of female sexuality in the late nineteenth century, is highly significant in this context. Glamour can be broadly defined as sexualised beauty, but it is a type of beauty in which the erotic is enhanced and heightened by the use of artifice. In the case of the theatre, actresses were not only glamorised by makeup and costume but lit in such a way as to accentuate their 'particularity'. It was the actresses who starred in

West End theatre who had the greatest caché as fashionable icons, and their dress both on and off stage was imitated and admired. Barbara Worsley Gough wrote of these women, who were described as professional beauties, that 'Their photographs bloomed in the shop windows, their faces were as familiar to the public as the faces of film stars today, and when they went to the theatre people stood on their seats to see them as they entered'.[13] Actresses such as Gabrielle Ray, Gertie Millar, Lilie Elsie and Zena and Phyllis Dare[14] were central to this iconography (Figure 2.2). In the early 1900s, the Gaiety Theatre was particularly significant in its identification with a highly fashionable female ideal, as embodied in actresses such as Gaby Deslys, who Cecil Beaton described after seeing her in his childhood: 'as the first creature of artificial glamour I ever knew about, one of that species of rare erotica'.[15] Beaton saw Deslys as 'a key transitional figure – a successor to the grand Parisian coquettes of the nineties on the one hand, and since she was a theatrical figure, the precursor of a whole school of glamour that was to be exemplified twenty years later by Marlene Dietrich ...'.[16] The designer Lucile was very much involved with dressing the 'Gaiety girls', including Gaby Deslys, both on and off stage. William Macqueen Hope observed, when reflecting on the period,

> The Gaiety stage door was indeed the gate way to romance. The Girls gilded the evening hours with loveliness as they approached it, and lit up the night, especially for their escorts, when they left after the show. To know a

Figure 2.2: Miss Marie Studholme, Miss Gabrielle Ray, Miss Zena Dare.
Postcard. London. Own collection.

Gaiety Girl, to take her out, that was a caché about town. The girls adorned the restaurants to which they were taken. Some of the most beautiful had their table reserved and were treated like queens.[17]

Gaiety girls were pursued by 'stage-door Johnnies', aristocrats and men-about-town for whom such women represented the highest ideal in femininity.

The Gaiety Theatre also presented reviews, which were very much aligned to fashion, and this was a key site in the promotion of new trends. *Our Miss Gibbs* was a production in which fashion was a central element in the creation of a theatrical spectacle.

There were magnificent dresses in *Our Miss Gibbs*. In the White City scene, the hats worn by the show girls alone cost sixty guineas each. They were brought down for every performance from the famous hat shop, Maison Lewis, and experts from the shop put them on the girls, standing afterwards in the wings to take them off and repack and return them to the shop again, ready for the next day … The effect of that fashion parade was superb.[18]

Magazines such as *Lady's Realm* were punctuated by studio photographs of both actresses and aristocrats, and a number of actresses who became aristocrats by marriage. The identities of actress and society beauty were those which represented the most desirable ideal for female readers, and which were strongly identified with fashionability. The identity combined the status of the established social order with a more commercial and modern idiom. These women were financially independent, and represented a kind of emancipation, although underpinned by extreme conventionality in dress and appearance. In 1892, *The Lady* began to carry a column 'Dress on the London Stage', and although this particular text quickly disappeared a number of similar columns were published across the popular press.[19] The readership of *The Lady* was at this point, as it still is, essentially upper-middle class and aristocratic. The London stage became a site for the marketing of commodities, and Maria Corelli 'claimed that such merchandising represented a cynical collusion of stage, shop and society press'.[20] Prominent fashion designers, including Worth, were involved in dressing plays from the 1880s, and this process escalated and reached its height in the early 1900s.

Lucile's career had initially developed in the context of this milieu, and her work is particularly interesting in relation to our concerns about the construction of femininity and fashion in this period. She opened her first premises in Old Burlington Street, Mayfair in 1895, and was a woman of extremely useful social and family connections, which ensured that she received the patronage of a wealthy and fashionable clientele. She worked at times on ideas for her designs with her sister, the writer Elinor Glyn, whose popular and scandalous 'bodice-ripping' novels reflected and shaped changing sexual mores. They shared a taste for glamour and the exotic, and it is interesting to look at their respective careers as representing the development of a new sensibility in female consumption, one in which desire and pleasure were mediated through changing arenas in cultural production. Lucile had become Lady Lucy Duff Gordon in the early 1900s. She and her sister had grown up in Jersey, and had as children encountered Lily Langtry, whose father was the Dean of Jersey, and who was at the beginning of her public career. Langtry, who in later life became a client of the House of Lucile, impressed both sisters with her distinctive elegance and desire for success. Elinor Glyn later became a close friend of Daisy Warwick, another mistress of Edward VII.[21] The close relationships between the fashionable and the authors of fashion in Britain was very clear in this period. It is also the case that, like Lily Langtry, Elinor Glyn and Lucile were both self-made women who, through social net-working and self-promotion, developed highly successful careers at a time in which it was still difficult for women to be effective in the public sphere.

Although Lucile had begun her career as a designer in the 1890s, she only became internationally successful in the 1900s, and at that time claimed to be the first designer to display her work on live models rather than mannequins.[22] Her designs represent a transitional phase in *haute couture*, and a new engagement with idioms and themes in the wider popular culture. The taste of the *nouveau riche*, of which Lucile and Elinor Glyn were part, were represented in Lucile's designs through the ostentation in their use of extravagantly luxurious fabrics and risqué styling. Some of Lucile's fashion shows were organised in co-operation with her sister, and these were themed to conform to the ideals of romanticism and sensuality to which they both subscribed and which can be identified in popular theatre, writing and the culture of the woman's magazine.

Kaplan and Stowell describe the fashion shows that Lucile held in her premises in the 1900s:

> The complex eroticism of her spectacles – working-class women dressed as society ladies promenading silently before an audience of middle- and upper-class men was further augmented by Lucile's decision to replace the numbers by which gowns had hitherto been identified with suggestive titles like 'Passion's thrall', 'Do you love me?' and a 'Frenzied song of amorous things'.[23]

The issue of class in this context is one which is to be found in the theatre itself, women of often indeterminate class being central to an entertainment attended predominantly by their social 'betters'. Lucile described her first mannequin parade held before an exclusive clientele, and at this point men were absent from the show:

> The Showroom was crowded. Princess Alice [the King's sister], the dearest, most human of all my royal patrons, sat near the front ... Ellen Terry was there, kind and thoughtful helping late arrivals to find their places; Lily Langtry, so beautiful that she made everyone turn to look at her ... It would be easier to

say in fact that society was present en masse, at least feminine society, for as yet no man had even thought of visiting such an entertainment.[24]

Cecil Beaton, in *The Glass of Fashion*, described theatrical costumes designed by Lucile as

> masterpieces of intricate workmanship ... Lucile worked with soft materials, delicately mingling them with bead and sequin embroidery, with cobweb lace insertions, true lovers knots, and garlands of minute roses. Her colour sense was so subtle that the delicacy of detail could hardly be seen at a distance, although the effect she created was of an indefinable shimmer.[25]

Lucile herself described such creations as her 'emotional dresses'. The impression created by these clothes was one of exaggeratedly feminine seductiveness. The clothes were part of a glamorous construction in which accretions of delicate fabrics and intricate decoration combined to create a mood that connected with the themes of eroticism and romance, which were also to be found in Elinor Glyn's fiction and later in her Hollywood screenplays.

Elinor Glyn has been quoted as having said that 'Romance is the glamour which turns the dust of everyday life into a golden haze'. The notion of the 'transforming magic' of fashion, which creates possibilities for women to transcend reality, is one which underpins the development of fashion markets in the twentieth century. Elinor Glyn's first novel had been published in 1906 and was titled *The Vicissitudes of Evangeline*,[26] but the book which made her name and fortune was the scandalous *Three Weeks*.[27] These books were 'bodice rippers' of a new type in incorporating the fashionable themes of romance and glamour with an overt eroticism. Considered shocking by moral arbiters of the day, *Three Weeks* describes the affair between an older married woman and a younger man. Their affair is presented in florid language, and reaches its romantic climax in Venice, where the protagonists consummate their love in a bower of lilacs and roses. Their affair ends in tragedy, but the heady sensuality and exoticism of the text connects it with other aspects of Edwardian culture. Both Lucile and Elinor Glyn travelled widely, and the latter in particular developed an affection for Egypt. In her novels one is reminded of the scenarios in paintings such as those of Lord Alfred Leighton and Lawrence Alma Tadema and a number of lesser-known painters of the late nineteenth century whose work shows seductive, diaphanously clad young women hedonistically luxuriating in Mediterranean sites surrounded by exotic blossoms. The bestselling perfumes at the turn of the century were based on the heavily eastern blend of sandalwood and tuberose which complemented the luxuriantly provocative character of Edwardian evening wear. This combination of escapism and romance was a common theme in the period, often underpinned by complex imperialist strategies of sexual displacement. The positioning of the openly sexual in sites in which women connoted 'otherness' allowed the voyeuristic Edwardian art lover the freedom of the gaze disassociated from connection with young women of the same race and class.

The work of both Elinor Glyn and Lucile was part of a cultural discourse centred around femininity and sexuality. It is an exploration of this discourse that offers a further understanding of the significance of the imagery concerned. From the mid-1880s there was a discernible shift in attitude in relation to sexuality, which we see most clearly in patterns of behaviour amongst sections of the ruling class and in some radical left-wing circles in the behaviour of figures such as Eleanor Marx and Edward Aveling, where the ideology of free love was articulated and enacted.[28] These changes, however, were realised very much on the margins of society, with the majority of the working and middle class still firmly adhering to conventional patterns of courtship and marriage, despite the challenges of cultural change. The court of Edward, Prince of Wales, with its sybaritic status, would seem to represent a reaction to the repressions of the mid-Victorian period, but it also reflected the aspirations of the new wealthy middle class whose prosperity was established at the height of industrialisation and who were now commercially and dynastically secure, able to enjoy a leisured existence, following the established recreational patterns of the aristocracy. This affluence had its basis in the spoils of empire, and was represented in luxury and excess. The clothes designed by Lucile and others were worn against a backdrop of extravagant opulence. Sensuality was an underlying theme in fashion and design, and this was complementary to the broader cultural mood. The elaborately decorated hats of the period, often adorned with feathers of exotic birds as well as fruits and flowers, were part of an imagery attached to a particular rarified and lavish representation of nature and to the idea of Britain as a cornucopia of the riches of the empire. Sir Osbert Sitwell commented on the London scene at the turn of the century:

> Never had there been such a display of flowers...a profusion of full blooded blossoms, of lolling roses and malmaisons, of gilded musical comedy baskets of carnations lent to some houses an air of exoticism. Never had Europe seen such mounds of peaches, figs nectarines and strawberries at all seasons, brought from their steamy tents of glass. Champagne bottles stood stacked on the sideboards and to the rich the show was free.[29]

This hedonism in which sexual licence played a part, was a key theme of the *fin de siècle,* and not only amongst the upper classes but also in aspects of artistic life. Aesthetes, most notably Oscar Wilde, embraced hedonism, claiming that, 'its aim indeed, was to experience itself, and not the fruits of experience, sweet or bitter as they may be...it was to teach man to concentrate himself upon the moments of that which is itself but a moment'.[30]

Wilde and his circle were described, in relation to their artistic identity and personal sexual preferences, as decadents. Elaine Showalter describes how 'in one sense, it was the pejorative label applied by the bourgeoisie to everything that seemed unnatural, artificial, and perverse'.[31] This concept of the artificial is one that we find across the cultural sites of literature and art, and we find evidence of it in fashion, where there is a tension between the 'made-upness' of parts of the imagery and the voluptuosity of the female body, which despite corseting connects in its implications of fertility with the idea of woman as 'natural'.

Wilde's openness about his own homosexuality and the stylised eroticism of the *Yellow Book* and other material produced by the aesthetes caused public outcry. Homosexuality had been identified and made illegal in 1885 by the Laboucherie Amendment to the Criminal Law Amendment Act. The trial and imprisonment of Wilde in 1895 marked a culminative point in the criminalisation and medicalisation of male homosexuality. As Elaine Showalter claims, 'Homosexuality became a medical problem, a pathology, even a disease; and medical and scientific speculations about homosexuality attempted to draw clear borderlines and labels...'.[32] It has been argued that a public anxiety about the dangers of homosexuality combined with further anxieties about female sexuality and emancipation were factors in a cultural imperative to clarify absolutely the boundaries between masculine and feminine, and that these factors contributed to the highly gendered nature of fashion and the fashionable female body in the period. Indeed Judith Butler, in *Gender Trouble*, an analysis of the work of Joan Riviere, refers to the possibility that 'femininity as masquerade is meant to deflect from male homosexuality...'.[33]

There were areas of cultural production in which women subverted the stereotype of feminine glamour. This was a period notable for its theatrical cross-dressing, with Vesta Tilley and other prominent female music-hall stars presenting as men (Figures 2.3 and 2.4). It has been suggested that performers such as Tilley were subverting the womanly stereotype in the only space in which such a challenge could be allowed, and it could be argued that dominant female representation was so excessively gendered that it demanded an extreme counterpoint. J.S. Bratton points out that Tilley in her private persona was an extremely 'womanly woman', and argues against interpreting this identity as having political implications. However, in the context of the apparent crisis around gender in this period, it is not unreasonable to interpret this phenomenon, which enjoyed a particular popularity in the 1890s and 1900s, as representing a significant space for a radical negotiation of culturally defined gendered roles.[34] There was an added complexity in the assumption of this seeming male identity in a period in which masculinity itself is in contention.

Figure 2.3: Miss Vesta Tilley, actress.
Postcard. London. Own collection.

Figure 2.4: Miss Vesta Tilley, actress. Postcard. London. Own collection.

In wearing a monocle, Tilley and Hettie King actually anticipated cross-dressing lesbian icons such as Una Trowbridge and Radclyffe Hall, and even later Marlene Dietrich and Madonna. Marjorie Garber cites the monocle as

> an ideal instance of the denaturalising of the sign in the context of gender and [homo]sexuality... An indication at once of supplement and lack, both instrumental and ornamental, connoting weakness and strength ...Simultaneously a signifier of castration... and empowerment.[35]

This implies the possible status of a third sex, separate and secure under the stage lights. As discussed at the beginning of the chapter, even conventional female fashion imagery was taken to an extreme that could be described as 'camp' in its artificiality, and there was a sense in which women in the context of fashion could be seen to be 'impersonating' women in a masquerade, facilitated by the developing apparatus of consumerism.

In the 1880s, Wilde had been strongly identified with a radical approach to dress, and had indeed lectured on aesthetic dress to audiences in Britain and America. Aesthetic dress for women did not challenge in any real way the conventions of femininity, but merely the structured artificiality of high fashion. Wilde straddled the worlds of society and art. In the 1880s, he developed an intense admiration for Lily Langtry, the epitome of new establishment glamour, whose beauty he admired despite her commitment to the restrictions of corseting and *haute couture*. Langtry, as already established, was an immensely popular figure, but she was also pivotal in the development of a new type of femininity, which while detached from the political idealism of the 'New Woman', was ultimately identified by entrepreneurialism and financial independence. In her twenties, while married to Ned Langtry, she had a succession of affairs with prominent society figures, including Edward VII and other luminaries. The new morality of the later nineteenth century allowed her to be accepted in this role, even to the point of being presented at court to Queen Victoria. However, after the birth of her daughter Jeanne and financial difficulties, she developed a career in the theatre that she continued into her sixties, and which placed her in popularity, if not talent, alongside Sarah Bernhardt.

Leonore Davidoff states that 'In sociological terms Society is an ever-changing status group based on communal lifestyles. The ever-changing rules of fashion become an element in control by such groups...'.[36] The everyday lives of the fashionable elite to which Langtry, Lucile and Elinor Glyn aspired were divided between properties in town and country, with country-house parties creating, it seems, the most opportunities for sexual recreation in the form of extramarital affairs. Travel abroad, to spas and resorts, was another part of the social year. 'As political life is segregated from social activity, Society functions came to be regarded simply as a way of life, pleasure as an end in itself...'.[37] The rituals of the leisured class made for the necessity for endless changes of costume, clothes for outdoors, indoors, sport, motoring, and for formal dinners and balls. These various events and functions created new and expanding markets in clothing and an increasing outlay on fashion for those wealthy enough to be part of the season.

In this moneyed arena, an engagement in relatively open sexual adventures by the Prince of Wales and his circle, far from resulting in notoriety for the women involved, in the case of Langtry, Alice Keppel and Daisy Warwick only increased their status and acceptance within society. Daisy, Lady Warwick had met Edward in 1883, and remained his 'favourite' until the mid-1890s, when she was succeeded by the society beauty Alice Keppel. Both women were known to Edward's wife Princess Alexandra.[38] My own great-grandfather remembered as a boy in the 1870s seeing Edward and Lily Langtry together, with seeming disregard for public opinion, at a local hotel in Purfleet in Essex, where they would regularly weekend after sailing down the Thames in Edward's yacht.[39] This shift in sensibility in relation to sexual behaviour and tolerance of erotic adventure by mature women in a particular social milieu could obviously be read as a reaction to the over-repressive conditions of the earlier nineteenth century, and part of the pleasure-led nature of contemporary experience within the moneyed class. However, other issues were involved, a significant factor being advances in contraception for women.

The development of effective contraception for women had been in process from as early as the 1820s, but it was from the 1880s that advertisements for female contraceptives were placed in certain women's magazines and health manuals.[40] The issue of birth control was highly contentious, and the publication of directives by doctors, often attached to the Malthusian League, such as Arthur Albutt's *The Wife's Handbook*, published in 1887. This publicised contraceptive measures for the poor and the advantages of the diaphragm in 'the possibility of its use without the inconvenience or knowledge of the husband'.[41] Such books were considered threatening to public morals, with anxieties centring around the possibility of information reaching the young unmarried lower classes.

The issue of class is obviously one of crucial importance here, with the middle and upper classes having access to information and products that were officially withheld from the lower classes for moral reasons. The emphasis in the advertisements for contraceptives in middle-class magazines was in improving efficacy, particularly in the case of the diaphragm. This sophisticated methodology would obviously make for an increased security in sexual activity for women. The fact that these methods were publicised within a particular milieu would also ensure that men of the same class were aware of this potentially liberating apparatus. Just as the much-heralded introduction of the contraceptive pill was arguably a factor in some complex renegotiation in female identity in fashion in the mid- to late 1960s, so the implications of a degree of sexual autonomy for certain constituencies of women could have been instrumental in some of the changes in the fashionable female ideal in the late nineteenth and early twentieth centuries.

There was a growing and conflicting literature on female sexuality from the 1880s onwards. Female sexuality was a subject of enormous contention in a period in which the subject of sexuality itself became part of a wide discourse across sites medical, social, political and cultural. In the 1880s and 1890s, events such as the Contagious Diseases Acts,[42] Stead's 'Maiden Tribute to Modern Babylon'[43] and the 'Ripper' murders in Whitechapel created a climate in which attitudes to female sexuality became part of a debate engaged in by feminists, social reformers, politicians and others. Significant attempts to engage with the subject had been made by the late 1880s, to allow for an acknowledgement of female sexual nature in a number of medical texts. For instance, Dr Elizabeth Blackwell, in her book *The Human Element in Sex* (1885), went to great lengths to stress that female sexual desire was as strong as that of men.[44] However, many women as well as men were opposed to these developments. There was particular concern from 'Purity and Vigilance' organisations, to which some feminists were attached, which believed in the ideology of the 'womanly woman', wife, mother and arbiter of sexual morality.

It was at this time that the new subject of sexology was developing, initiated by Richard von Kraft Ebbing, who published his *Pscychopathia Sexualis* in Vienna in 1886, in the same city as Fleiss and Freud were working on early psychoanalytic theory. Havelock Ellis, the British sexologist, published the first volume of his *Studies in the Psychology of Sex* a decade later. Although this work did not have a direct impact on thinking until the early twentieth century, it nevertheless represented a shift, no matter how problematically, in the way in which female sexuality was considered. Lynn Segal claims that both pioneers of sex research

> equated sex and gender, and saw male and female sexuality as fundamentally opposed; the one aggressive and forceful the other responsive and maternal. As a sexual and social reformer Ellis upheld the possibility and importance of female sexual pleasure…the only female pleasure which could be recognised was one responsive to male initiative.[45]

There were those within feminism and radical politics, such as Olive Schreiner, who questioned his position, but certainly majority opinion across a range of sites medical, sociological and latterly psychoanalytical concurred with Ellis. Thus the potential for female sexual pleasure was formally established, but with the Darwinian order of male supremacy still implicit. This is the concept that dominates the novels of Elinor Glyn and many other examples of fiction for women, and it can also be seen in clothes, such as those designed by Lucile, for the seductive married woman. The ideal is one of passionate romantic love, best situated within marriage.

The conjunction of passion and romance was identified with the older woman, and it was the older woman who was the most fashionable type of the 1890s. In the novel *Three Weeks*, Elinor Glyn's heroine is an older woman admired by the young Paul Verdayne for her sophistication and experience. Valerie Steele quotes Lucile, who identified the bias of fashion towards the older woman: 'As a general rule the fashions were created for older women, and were only adapted for the *jeune fille*, often unsuitably at that'.[46] Certainly during the whole of this period the majority of young unmarried women of the middle and upper classes were still chaperoned and expected to retain virginity until marriage. The *fin de siècle* is a rare period in representing the matron, and that includes women well into their forties, the epitome of the seductive. The new acceptance of cosmetics and hair colourants added to the possibility of women looking younger for longer. The overtly seductive mature woman became highly acceptable in a climate in which sexuality was facilitated by new contraceptive technologies, and pleasure and display were central to fashionable behaviour. In a period rife with anxieties about female sexuality and burgeoning female power, it is interesting that it was the more experienced and possibly more sexually assertive older woman who was central in fashionable imagery. It could be argued that her assumed married status placed her safely within the patriarchal order.

The relationship between morality and fashion was one which was of great concern to commentators throughout the nineteenth century. Mrs Hawies, who wrote on fashion in the 1870s, was influenced in her ideas by an engagement with the principles of the aesthetic movement and a concern with an appropriate level of decorum in the dress of middle-class women. She wrote widely on the subject of fashion, and claimed that

> in nothing, are character and perception so insensibly but inevitably displayed as in dress, and taste. Dress is the second self, a dumb self, yet almost eloquent expositor of the person. Dress bears the same relation to the body as speech does to the brain; and therefore dress may be called the speech of the body.[47]

This analysis prefigures what Elizabeth Wilson was to write a century later, when claiming that 'Dress is the cultural metaphor for the body, it is the material with which we "write" or "draw" a representation of the body into our cultural context'.[48] There continued to be, in the dress reform movement, amongst hygienists and some feminists, an ongoing interrogation of female dress codes as the nineteenth century came to an end. Their concerns were heightened in response to the increasing promotion of fashion in the popular media.

There were a range of women's magazines at the turn of the century in which fashion was the central element in the construction of the feminine. Interestingly, as Margaret Beetham observes even magazines such as *Home Chat*, with its working- and lower-middle-class readership, had fashion pages edited by journalists whose aristocratic *noms de plumes* linked them to the more upmarket *The Lady* and *Lady's Realm* and underlined the identification of fashion with Edwardian society.[49] It was in these magazines that the role of the fashion writer as interpreter of and advisor on fashion developed. In the early twentieth century, Mrs Eric Pritchard, another friend of Daisy Warwick, and one who moved in the same aristocratic circles as Lucile and her sister, was a prominent commentator on fashion. Her writing in *The Lady* and *Lady's Realm* was very much a part of the dominant fashion scene, although unusual perhaps in its tone and promotion of fashion as an agent of eroticism and romance. Her writing displays a thorough engagement with consumer pleasures and a particularly Edwardian perspective on the construction of femininity through clothing and self-presentation. Mrs Pritchard wrote a regular column on London and Paris fashions in *Lady's Realm* in the 1900s, where she identified new developments in style and recommended designers and retail outlets where fashionable purchases might be made. As life in Edwardian society required a number of outfits for any given day, fashion markets rapidly expanded.

Advertisements in women's magazines reinforced the representation of fashion and the female body: 'Womanly beauty was simultaneously guaranteed as natural and – like her health – always threatened and dependent on the constant work of construction and artifice'.[50] Advertisements for corsets, hair dyes, cosmetics and the other beauty apparatus opened up a world in which the construction of the feminine through commodities became identified with female duty. It became the responsibility of women to recreate them-selves in the form presented on the fashion and society pages. In a section in *Lady's Realm*, 'Health and Beauty for Hair' 'Narcissa' instructs: 'There should be three [brushes] on the dressing-table of every woman who values her appearance (and what really nice woman does not?)'.[51] Here we see established the rules by which the feminine must be shaped.

In her book *The Cult of Chiffon*,[52] Mrs Pritchard had likened the pursuit of personal beauty to a religion, and particularly extolled the seductive function of lingerie in marriage. Anxieties about venereal disease, which were represented in the plays of Ibsen and in novels such as *The Yolk*,[53] drove the middle class towards a stronger imperative for fidelity. As has been seen, however, some did not share these concerns, and obviously – although Mrs Pritchard may not have condoned it – alluring lingerie as well as other elements of cosmetic disguise provided an impetus for extramarital as well as marital love.

There is a sense in which in Edwardian high fashion the distinction between under- and outerwear is blurred, particularly in evening dress. *Lady's Pictorial* of December 1895 carries an illustration of a highly elaborate and ultra-feminine evening dress from the Dickens and Jones catalogue across the page from an advertisement for trousseau lingerie characterised by the same 'frou-frou' glamour.[54] In the 1900s, Lucile had, according to Kaplan and Stowell, a part of her premises in Burlington Road called the Rose Room in which lingerie was shown to an exclusive clientele by appointment only. She designed transparent nighties, lace knickers and chiffon petticoats, and these were complementary to her clothing designs.[55] Pale colours, such as mauves, whites and creams, combined with delicate embroidery and decolletage created a look in outerwear that referred closely to the look of lingerie in the period and reinforced the idea of fashion as seduction. The theme of the veil, which recurs in art and literature at this time, can also be seen in fashion in this layering of fine and translucent materials. The idea of 'woman's mystery' as part of her armoury against sexual betrayal and abandonment is one that is reinforced by these images.

Elaine Showalter, in discussing the theme of the veil in her book *Sexual Anarchy, Gender and Culture at the Fin de Siècle*, describes how 'Figures of female sexuality at the *fin de siècle* are frequently represented as exotic and veiled'.[56] She discusses the significance of the oriental woman, who, behind the veil of purdah, stood as a figure of sexual secrecy and inaccessibility in the 1880s and 1890s.[57] The paintings of Alma Tadema, Albert Moore and Lord Alfred Leighton prominently represent the veiled oriental or Eastern Mediterranean woman dressed diaphanously and posed seductively in settings suggesting the harem. The way in which these paintings touch on the exotic and theatrical nature of Edwardian taste, and their significance in the framing of sexuality, have been already touched on. The models in these paintings are young, Junoesque and uncorseted. From the 1870s, British painting had been increasingly influenced by French orientalism and that such openly erotic material was placed in the 'other' world of the East obviously allowed these paintings to be consumed without their content seeming to compromise the status of the proper young women of late-nineteenth-century England.[58] In magazines of various kinds, fashion articles were placed alongside profiles of popular artists, Tadema and his circle being prominent in this regard. Cassell's *Family Magazine* contained popular fiction, often of a romantic nature, an illustrated section entitled 'Chit-Chat on Dress' and occasional material on art and design. The integration of popular painting with fashion and romantic fiction in these magazines was part of a broad discourse on femininity that informed middle-class taste.

The clothing worn in paintings such as those by Tadema, minimal though it was, did in some ways connect to the loose, diaphanous and unstructured nature of fashionable items such as the tea gown and more closely the peignoir or negligee. The veil was

> associated with female sexuality and with the veil of the hymen. The veil thus represented feminine chastity and modesty; in rituals of the nunnery, marriage, or mourning, it concealed sexuality. Furthermore science and medicine had traditionally made use of sexual metaphors which represented 'Nature' as a woman to be unveiled by the man who seeks her secrets.[59]

Aubrey Beardsley's illustrations of Oscar Wilde's veiled *Salome* published in 1893 appear ostensibly to concern growing preoccupations with the perceived dangers of female sexuality, and implicitly the process of female seduction. However, Marjorie Garber identifies this site as transvestite masquerade; indeed there is a famous photograph which is claimed to be of Oscar Wilde himself dressed as Salome. Garber states

> that because human sexuality is constructed through repression, the signifier of desire cannot be represented directly, but only under a veil. Taken together, these somewhat abstract formulations about the dancer, the dance, and the veiled phallus, tell the story of the power of Salome – and the reason why the removal of the last veil is the sign of her death. For when the veil is lifted, what is revealed is the transvestite – the deconstruction of the binary, the riddle of culture.[60]

The fact that high fashion under the exhortations of the likes of Mrs Eric Pritchard and Lucile was so overtly concerned with seduction, and that veiling played such a central role in the structuring of lingerie and outer-wear, created an image of a highly fetishised character intimating complex sexual anxieties as well as pleasures in a period beset with panic over definitions of both sexuality and gender. Elaine Showalter, in discussing the veil in relation to art, refers to Freud, who 'interpreted the myth of Medusa's head as an allegory of the veiled woman, whose unshielded gaze turns men to stone'.[61] A postcard of the actress Marie Studholme from 1904, posing glamorously in veiled Eastern style, illustrates the cultural crossover of these themes from art to fashion and popular entertainment (Figure 2.5).

The layers of chiffon, so beloved of Mrs Pritchard, refer to this process of veiling, and were intended to combine the function of modesty with allure. Danger was diffused by the emphasis on delicate fabrics and pale colours that refer more to the nursery in some ways than to the night. The complex identity of female sexuality, with its emphasis on married love, and the combining therefore of sex and propriety, makes this ambiguous form of dress and possibly undress particularly apposite. Interestingly, the other heyday of the negligee was in the 1950s, when similar axes of innocence and experience and the social imperative of marital sexual contentment prevailed, despite increasing possibilities for female emancipation.

The ideal female body in fashion in the 1890s and early twentieth century was significantly larger than the ideal of the 1860s and 1870s. Lucile describes her fashion models as 'six foot of perfect symmetry ... Not one of them weighed under eleven stone and several of them weighed considerably more. They were big girls with fine figures'.[62] From the 1880s, the ideal female figure had been gradually increasing in both height and weight. There is a sense that the female body itself became a site of ostentatious consumption in its ampleness, a tribute to good nutrition, and indeed in the case of the aristocracy to an extremely lavish diet. From the 1870s, cheap American corn had been available in Britain, as well as refrigerated meat and fruit from the colonies, improving nutrition across the classes by the 1890s.[63] Vita Sackville-West describes the eating habits of the aristocracy in her novel *The Edwardians*:

> Those meals! Those endless extravagant meals in which they all indulged all year round! Sebastian wondered how their constitutions and figures could stand it: then he remembered that in summer they went as a matter of course to Homberg or Marienbad. Really there was little difference between Marienbad and the vomitarium of the Romans. How strange that eating should play so important a part in social life.[64]

By the 1890s, images of women across social class indicated the fashion for curves. In London and other cities there was a proliferation of restaurants and cafes in which middle- and upper-middle-class women could enjoy

Figure 2.5: Miss Marie Studholme, actress. Postcard. James Bacon and Sons, Newcastle-upon-Tyne. Own collection.

eating in a newly public way, as they began to penetrate unchaperoned the spaces in cities that had previously been predominantly masculine.[65] The department store offered women the opportunity to enjoy the pleasures of consumption unchaperoned, and also to meet with friends to eat and relax. Selfridges, along with other department stores, had a restaurant in the 1900s that covered a whole floor, and catered for a mainly female clientele. Photographs of customers in these restaurants show women elaborately dressed up whilst engaging in calorific teatime rituals.

The dimensions of this ideal body appear anathemic to theories that suggest that the maternal and the sexual in combination are incompatible within patriarchy. Griselda Pollock, discussing imageries of peasant women in paintings of the 1880s, describes that particular genre as a site in which 'there are traces of failed repression, traces which make legible the uneven sacrificial process by which masculinity was formed in its particular relations to lost maternal bodies created in the social division of childcare at the time'.[66] Such women were allowed to suggest those repressed characteristics in this imagery because they are 'other' to the bourgeois ideal, and identified with the servant class, and the representation of the female body in these paintings is fraught with Oedipal tensions at once aggressive and idealising, the latter identity being evident in 'the size and physicality of the body's lap, buttocks and torso as signs of comfort'.[67] The scale and voluptuousness of the fashionable female body at the turn of the century, with such emphasis on breasts and buttocks, could also be read in terms of maternal comfort and of perhaps a renegotiation of class and identity in the period. The uxorious scale of the middle-class ideal in the 1890s and 1900s is in stark contrast to the delicate femininity that represented refinement and breeding in mid-century. Physical characteristics that would have been considered vulgar to the mid-Victorian era, alluding to the peasant class described by Pollock, were now considered desirable. There was a stress in the 1890s and 1900s across a range of discourse on the concept of the 'womanly woman', for whom motherhood is a defining role. This identity was culturally dominant in the face of escalating feminism, and there were at the end of the nineteenth century new types of imagery showing middle-class and aristocratic women as mothers, seemingly enjoying this aspect of their experience.

Paintings such as those by Isaac Snowman[68] show elegantly dressed women with young children (Figure 2.6). Edwardian photographs of aristo-cratic subjects often present the elaborately coiffured mother holding her offspring, and these punctuate the text in magazines such as The Lady, and are unlike many earlier Victorian photographic portraits of the ruling class, which emphasised family rather than motherhood alone. These images represent a sanitised and glamorous form of motherhood removed through developing techniques of femininity, removed by class from the degree of animal physicality in the peasant images discussed by Pollock. The glamour of the clothing and the implicit seductiveness of the maternal subject, along with a voluptuous body, combined to create an image in which the mechanisms of the Oedipal complex can be seen at play in the fetishistic nature of the cosmeticised and corseted female body, yet with a scale of body that inevitably infers reproductive power. It could be argued that in a period in which anxieties about the New Woman, the masculinised woman, were so powerful that somehow there was slippage in dominant imagery, allowing the maternal to be integrated with the sexual in an imagery that confronted the 'emasculating' presence of the modern woman.

For the affluent consumer of high fashion, the body was encased in highly structured corseting that exerted a sheath-like control. The function of the corset and the aptly named sheath dress in late-nineteenth-century fashion can be read in a similar way. Fashion, like art in this period, was concerned with the 'containment and regulation of the female body'. Interestingly, in fashionable imageries, especially photographic ones, these attempts to control and contain within the schema of fashion are inadvertently confounded by the voluptuousness of the body and the impression of a bursting, overflowing femaleness which results from the process of tight lacing. The distortive emphasis on breasts and buttocks stresses the female

Figure 2.6: Isaac Snowman, painting. *Windsor Magazine*, 10 June 1904.

body's margins and places some of these fashionable images outside contemporary tropes of female containment in visual culture.

In *The Edwardians*, Vita Sackville-West describes the process of dressing the Duchess, a character based on Alice Keppel, for a ball in the presence of her children, Sebastian and Viola. The image she describes is one of sexual allure but also refinement, and connects with other representations, literary and visual, of the aristocratic female as opposed to the fashionable beauty:

> These inner mysteries of his mother's toilet were unknown to Sebastian, but Viola knew well what was going on...her mother would rise, and standing in her chemise, would allow the maid to fit the long stays of pink coutil, heavily boned around her hips and slender figure, fastening the busk down the front after many adjustments; then the suspenders would be clipped to the stockings, then the lacing would follow, beginning at the waist and travelling gradually down.[69]

The paintings of John Singer Sargent, prominent academician and society portraitist, offer a particular perspective on the construction of an aristocratic ideal of beauty at the *fin de siècle*. His paintings represent a stylisation of dominant late-nineteenth-century notions of beauty and fashionability. They were mostly commissioned by the husbands or fathers of those portrayed, and therefore offer us an interesting interpretation of a certain type of female identity at this time, which is at variance with many of the photographic images that we have of fashionable women of this class, who appear to be much more worldly, sophisticated and voluptuous. There is a paleness, an untouchability about the women painted by Sargent, a sensuality washed by colours identified with innocence, thus neutralising some of the more overtly sexual connotations of their glamorous and often revealing clothing.

In a painting such as 'The Aecherson Sisters', 1902,[70] Sargent presents us with a particular vision that refers tangentially to the exotic in the large garlanded urn and peach tree which form the background, but in its painterly restraint and the dignified elegance of the young women portrayed it retains a Gainsborough-like Englishness. A characteristic of this painting and other subjects, such as Lady Agnew, painted 1892–3 (Figure 2.7),[71] is the elegant and healthy look of the sitters, as if Sargent was pointing to some inherent eugenic superiority to be found in the privileged elite. Height, particularly in the case of the first painting, is emphasised, with the impression that these women are nearing six feet tall. These are younger women than many of those photographed in society pages, and they are not as curvaceous as many other representations of women at the time in other types of painting, and in photographs and illustrations. They are dressed in fashionably exquisite pale silks and satins, which combined with their apparent *hauteur* sets them apart from images of women in more popular iconography. Sargent also executed a series of paintings of mothers and children from the same aristocratic and wealthy milieu, in which age difference is minimised by careful brushwork, and the desirability of the older woman placed beyond question.

Deborah Cherry and Jane Beckett refer to the whiteness of female imagery at this time, and to how such images speak of British imperialism and the notion of the superiority of white women of a certain class.[72] This can be seen in much dominant fashion imagery, in which there was an emphasis on pale colours and delicate fabrics, but it is particularly evident in those representations of fashionability such as Sargent's portraits which eschew those aspects of femininity that connote earthiness and fecundity, presenting instead a streamlined and untouchable identity that counters the increasing accessibility of images of the upper classes through the expanding media.

There are obvious differences in style and presentation which define women in this period in relation to class. It is clear from postcards and photographs showing highly popular working actresses and music-hall stars, such as Marie Studholme, Jessie Preston and Marie Lloyd, that these icons of a lower class had a more relaxed and less formal image than society

Figure 2.7: John Singer Sargent, *Lady Agnew*, 1895.
Reproduced by permission of the Scottish National Gallery.

beauties, and even than more prestigious and stylish actresses of the period, such as Constance Collier and Gaby de Lisle. They are loosely corseted, and wear clothes that are more colourful and unstructured. They share the voluptuousness of the fashionable ideal, but appear to be more natural in the way in which they present themselves to the camera and the viewer. Marie Studholme, of whom there are many images on contemporary postcards, is shown wearing clothes that lack the smooth finished quality of high fashion. There is a sense of improvisation in details of clothing, an excess of lace and embroidery, which even by Edwardian standards appear over decorative. There is artifice in the obvious use of cosmetics and hair dyes here, but the intimacy of the facial expressions and relaxed deportment suggest an open engagement with sexuality that, to quote Marie Lloyd, suggests that 'a little bit of what you fancy does you good'. These images are every bit as imposing as those of women in high-fashion imagery, but are less formal, and so in some ways appear more modern (Figures 2.8 and 2.9).

In the early 1900s, the S-bend corset became a defining element in high fashion, creating a body shape which consisted of 'a large overhanging bosom, narrow waist and protruding hips and bottom'. This was the sartorial

Figure 2.8: Miss Ethel Oliver, actress.
Postcard. London. Own collection.

Figure 2.9: Miss Marie Studholme.
Postcard. London. Own collection.

equivalent of the art nouveau whiplash, and emphasised the 'magnificent daintiness'[73] of the mature fashion consumer. It was in this period that the phenomenon of the Gibson Girl emerged. Initially the Gibson Girl was a concept marketed by Charles Dana Gibson, an American illustrator, and represented a younger, more athletic, physical type than that which dominated the established fashion arena. Jennifer Craik refers to her as 'the first truly international role model', as her image was marketed worldwide.[74] The idea was used to sell a range of products, and was translated into theatrical review. This image ran alongside the more conventional high fashion imagery, and offered for younger women a look that, in its relative informality and slight masculinisation, intimated the modernity emerging as a result of a changing climate of expanding educational and vocational opportunity for middle-class women. It is a fashion identity framed in a popular cultural milieu, and gained enormous popularity, indicating a shift in the locus of stylistic innovation, challenging the dominance of *haute couture* as the twentieth century moved on.

The *Windsor Magazine*, which contained a great deal of coverage of contemporary art and fiction, contained illustrations by artists such as Penryhn Stanslaws that represented highly fashionable women in the manner of Gibson (Figure 2.10).[75] As Elizabeth Wilson states, 'The young woman of 1900 who bought a cheap Gibson Girl blouse, didn't just buy a blouse: she bought a symbol of emancipation, glamour and success'.[76] A poem by John Arbuthnott, 'To a Gibson Girl', published in the *Windsor Magazine* in 1904, expressed the way in which the image of the Gibson Girl was associated with independence and freedom, although here the writer suggests that it may have been a case of image over reality:

> Simulating ice and snow;
> Proud impassive, haughty, cold,
> From your satin slippered toe
> To each tress of wayward gold!
>
> Pouting-lipped complexity;
> Daphne gay in crepe de Chine;
> Softer-souled Euryale
> Sedately gowned in etamine!
>
> Child of old Deucalion,
> Mocked by all this modern pomp;
> Aphrodite, full of fun;
> Juno aching for a romp!

Figure 2.10: Penryhn Stanslaws, illustration in the style of Charles Dana Gibson. *Windsor Magazine*, June 1904.

Dreaming-eyed, unmoved, austere;
Towering queen of dignity
To a hoodwinked world my dear,
But imposter unto me.

For I know you – I alone –
Laughing wayward child of sun,
And impulsive, overgrown
Girl and angel, all in one![77]

The actress Camille Clifford – who became the theatrical personification of the Gibson Girl taking London by storm in the early century with her stage performances – is often photographed in extremely structured evening dress, in which her ample figure is tight laced and conforms strongly to the established high-fashion S-bend rather than the more attenuated body shape that characterises Gibson's drawings.[78] There is an interesting contrast between the original ideal that influenced some contemporary fashion illustrators and the more familiar reality of early-twentieth-century female iconography, as represented in photographs of Clifford herself (Figure 2.11).

Figure 2.11: Miss Camille Clifford. Postcard.
London. Own collection.

Paul Poiret, the French couturier who began his career in Paris in 1903, had, like Gibson, conceived of a more youthful and athletic type as the ideal model for his designs. However, this change in emphasis to a slimmer and much less structured silhouette had, it seems, little impact on the dress of the wealthy and fashionable in Britain until several years later. Osbert Sitwell wrote that in 1907,

> For the first time for many decades ... At Ascot, and on the lawns of garden parties, it was to be noticed that women had at last begun to shed once more the multitude of their garments, had left behind the veilings and feather boas in which we saw them wrapped at Lord's, and were now clad, skin-deep, in tight silks, were sheathed in satin, or wore slit skirts and silver anklets. For the world took its note from musical comedy rather than from the immense tragedies that were being prepared in the wings to replace it, and the Production of *Les Merveilleuses* at Daly's in November 1906 had introduced, or at any rate popularised, Directoire dresses.[79]

The influence of the theatre on changing fashions is again evident here.

The significance of the ideal female body type up to this point is complex. I have discussed the changes in attitude to consumption, sexuality and birth control as factors that could contribute to the more overtly seductive nature of fashion and the emphatically feminine body. The New Woman, who engaged with feminist ideology and was to identify with suffragism, might be assumed to offer a counterpoint to the imagery with which we are concerned. However, the issue of 'womanhood' and the ways in which it was represented often overlapped with conventional imageries. Rosemary Betterton describes how it was necessary as in the case of the WSPU[80] 'to represent true womanliness to counter the popular image of the "shrieking sisterhood". The fashionable dress of the suffragettes, even if wildly impractical in a violent fracas, implied conformity to contemporary dress codes and emphasised their femininity'.[81] Banners used in parades by the suffragettes represented heroic images of women, such as Joan of Arc, who shared aspects of the physical monumentality of the female ideal of the period and yet, as Rosemary Betterton points out, was 'sheathed' in armour, corseted in steel, a strategy in this site for distancing femininity from the corporeal and representing ideas of strength, invincibility and virtue. Marina Warner, in 'Monuments and Maidens',[82] identifies the ways in which emotion and virtue are written on the female body in monuments such as the Statue of Liberty at this time. The body as represented in these monuments, is one characterised by emphatically classical proportions inferring qualities of moral strength and maternal protectiveness.

The classical ideal, as represented in painting and statuary, was of Venus-like proportions, with less emphasis on breasts and hips than in some more popular cultural sites. The ideal female body which dominated fashion iconography at the *fin de siècle* was Junoesque, and in some images touched on the exaggerated proportions of earth goddesses, with breasts and buttocks emphasised and celebrated.[83] The relationship between fertility and sexuality is extant in fashionable female imagery, especially between 1890 and 1906, in which, as already stated, there was a preoccupation with the role of woman as mother, and although younger women were entering the world of work many older women, especially in the middle and upper classes, were still identified by their marital status and their child-bearing capacities. Fashion provided a pleasurable site for the display of status. Clothes may have been heavy, but the layers of silks and soft fabrics that underpinned the final effect must have been sensual to wear. Debates around corseting identify both the restrictive and harmful aspects of the practice as well as the potentially autoerotic and pleasurable. The fashion for voluptuosity allowed for an open enjoyment of food, despite the beginnings in the early twentieth century of advice on healthier eating. Women enjoyed exercise in walking and sports, but the imperative was towards good health and physical strength rather than slimness as an end in itself. There are elements here that contrast with later-twentieth-century discipline in relation to the body, and the associated critical separation between fertility and sexuality.

Photographs of Edwardian women walking in the modern city of the early twentieth century reveal an interesting tension between the increasing angularity of buildings, the speed and bustle of the urban experience, and the extravagance and complexity of their dress and appearance. It was a period of enormous change. In domestic politics there was the rise of the Labour Party and the trades unions, as well as the escalation of the women's suffrage campaign. From the 1880s, there had been rumblings of dissent in the empire, and the establishment was under siege. In some ways the extravagance of fashion imagery could be read as the old order 'written on the female body'. These images of women are problematic, as they operated within a threatened but highly constraining patriarchal order. Many of these women, although privileged, were financially dependent and had limited choices in life. Some, however, were independent, and financially successful as we have seen in the cases of Lucile, her sister and others. They enjoyed certain pleasures without censure, and some were able to accept the reproductive aspects of their identity alongside the sexual, albeit under the constraints of a threatened but effective patriarchy. It has been argued that the fertile opulence of Edwardian womanhood represented a type of biological reductivism, but it represents something more complex than that, as this chapter has tried to establish. A century on, the sanitised and airbrushed imagery of contemporary fashion locks us into universal images of the sexualised teenage girl, and it is impossible for many of us to see ourselves or identify our experience of our bodies with what we see. Edwardian fashion imagery, despite its unwieldiness, speaks of a viscerality and a power attached to the combination of the sexual and reproductive which spilled over into the spaces of modernity. The photographs of these women challenge our contemporary expectations of femininity, and in their impact remind us perhaps of aspects of ourselves that have long been repressed in dominant cultural representation.

NOTES ON CHAPTER 2

1   T.J. Clark, *The Painting of Modern Life: Paris in the Art of Manet and His Followers* (London, Thames and Hudson), 1985, p.6, cited in Lisa Tickner, *The Spectacle of Women: Imagery in the Suffrage Campaign 1907–14*, (London, Chatto and Windus, London, 1987), p.151.

2   E. Ellen Leopold, 'The Manufacture of the Fashion System', in Juliet Ash and Elizabeth Wilson (eds), *Chic Thrills: A Fashion Reader* (London, Pandora, 1992), p.104.

3   Julian Robinson, *The Golden Age of Style* (London, Orbis, 1976), p.34.

4   Erika Diane Rappaport, *Shopping for Pleasure: Women in the Making of London's West End* (Princeton, Princeton University Press, 2000), p.163.

5   Ibid.

6   Robinson, *The Golden Age of Style*, p.32.

7   J. Mordaunt Crook, *The Rise and Fall of the Nouveaux Riches: Style and Status in Victorian and Edwardian Architecture* (London, John Murray, 1999), pp.258–9.

8   Griselda Pollock, *Vision and Difference: Femininity, Feminism and the Histories of Art* (London, Routledge, 1988), p.124.

9   Ibid., p.128.

10 Ibid.

11 Hilary and Mary Evans, *The Party that Lasted One Hundred Days: The Late Victorian Season, A Social Study* (London, MacDonald and Jane's, 1976), p.97.

12 Annette Kuhn, *The Power of The Image: Essays on Representation and Sexuality* (London, Routledge & Kegan Paul, 1985), p.12.

13 Barbara Worsley Gough, 'Fashions in London', in Katrina Rolley (ed.), *Fashion in Photographs 1900–1920* (London, Batsford, 1992), p.22.

14 J.B. Priestly, *The Edwardians* (London, Heinemann, 1970), p.69.

15 Cecil Beaton, *The Glass of Fashion* (London, Cassell, 1989), p.36.

16 Ibid.,p.38.

17 James Laver, *Edwardian Promenade* (London, Hulton, 1958), p.76.

18 Ibid.

19 Joel H. Kaplan and Sheila Stowell, *Theatre and Fashion: Oscar Wilde to the Suffragettes* (Cambridge, Cambridge University Press, 1994), p.8.

20 Ibid., p.28.

21 Theo Aronson, *The King in Love* (London, John Murray, 1988), p.209.

22 Beaton, *The Glass of Fashion*, p.34.

23 Kaplan and Sheila, *Theatre and Fashion*, p.8.

24 Lucile, Lady Duff Gordon, *Discretions and Indiscretions* (London, Jarrolds, 1932).

25 Beaton, *The Glass of Fashion*, p.78.

26 Elinor Glyn, *The Vicissitudes of Evangeline* (London, 1906).

27 Elinor Glyn, *Three Weeks* (London, Virago, 1996).

28 Yvonne Kapp, *Eleanor Marx: The Crowded Years 1884–1898* (London, Virago, 1976).

29 Simon Nowell Smith (ed.), *Edwardian England, 1901 to 1914* (London, Oxford University Press, 1964), p.35.

30 Oscar Wilde, *The Fortnightly Review*, London, March 1894.

31 Elaine Showalter, *Sexual Anarchy, Gender and Culture at the Fin de Siècle* (London, Bloomsbury, 1991), p.169.

32 Showalter, *Sexual Anarchy, Gender and Culture at the Fin de Siècle*, p.14.

33 Judith Butler, *Gender Trouble: Feminism and the Subversion of Identity* (London, Routledge, 1990), p.52.

34 J.S. Bratton, 'Irrational Dress', in Viv Gardener and Susan Rutherford (eds), *The New Woman and Her Sisters* (Hemel Hempstead, Harvester Wheatsheaf, 1992).

35 Marjorie Garber, *Vested Interests: Cross Dressing and Cultural Anxiety* (London, Penguin, 1993), p.154.

36 Leonore Davidoff, *The Best Circles* (London, Cresset Library, 1973), p 37.

37 Ibid., p.65.

38 Christopher Hibbert, *Edward VII: A Portrait* (London, Penguin, 1976), pp.159–69.

39 Charles Carr, great-grandfather of the author, Hilary Fawcett.

40 Lucy Bland, *Banishing the Beast: English Feminism and Sexual Morality 1885–1914* (London, Penguin 1995), p.194.

41 Bland, *Banishing the Beast*, p.137.

42 The Contagious Diseases Act 1869 had been imposed to prevent venereal diseases in the armed forces. Any woman who was assumed to be involved in prostitution could be detained against her will for up to three months.

43 Stead's 'Maiden Tribute to Modern Babylon', journalistic series published in 1885 by W.T. Stead on child prostitution, which caused moral outrage and contributed to the raising of the age of consent.

44 Patricia Branca, *Silent Sisterhood: Middle Class Women in the Victorian Home* (London, Croom Helm, 1975), p.126.

45 Lynn Segal, *Straight Sex: The Politics of Pleasure* (London, Virago, 1994), pp.76–7.

46 Valerie Steele, *Fashion and Eroticism: Ideals of Feminine Beauty from the Victorian Era to the Jazz Age* (Oxford, Oxford University Press, 1985), p.222.

47 Alison Gernsheim, *Victorian and Edwardian Fashion: A Photographic Survey* (New York, Dover Publications, 1983), p.66.

48 Ash and Wilson (eds), *Chic Thrills*, p.6.

49 Margaret Beetham, *A Magazine of Her Own: Domesticity and Desire in the Women's Magazine 1800–1914* (London, Routledge, 1996), p.195.

50 Ibid., p.151.

51 *Lady's Realm*, vol. xvi, May–October 1904, p.722.

52 Mrs Eric Pritchard, *The Cult of Chiffon* (London Grant Richards, 1902).

53 Lucy Bland, 'Sex and Morality', in Jane Beckett and Deborah Cherry (eds), *The Edwardian Era* (Oxford, Phaidon and Barbican Art Gallery, 1987), p.92.

54 *Lady's Pictorial*, vol. xxx, 14 December 1895, pp.14–15.

55 Kaplan and Stowell, *Theatre and Fashion*, p.39.

56 Elaine Showalter, *Sexual Anarchy: Gender and Culture at the Fin de Siècle* (London, Bloomsbury, 1991), p.144.

57 Ibid., p.145.

58 Alison Smith, *The Victorian Nude: Sexuality, Morality and Art* (Manchester, Manchester University Press, 1996).

59 Showalter, *Sexual Anarchy*, p.145.

60 Garber, *Vested Interests*, p.344.

61 Showalter, *Sexual Anarchy*, p.145.

62 Lady Duff Gordon, *Discretions and Indiscretions*, p.18.

63 Asa Briggs, *A Social History of England* (London, Book Club Associates, 1984), p.339.

64 Vita Sackville-West, *The Edwardians* (London, Virago, 1983).

65 Lynne Walker, 'Vistas of Pleasure: Women Consumers of Urban Space in the West End of London 1850–1900', in Clarissa Campbell Orr (ed.), *Women in the Victorian Art World* (Manchester, Manchester University Press, 1995).

66 Griselda Pollock, *Differencing the Canon: Feminist Desire and the Writing of Art's Histories* (London, Routledge, 1999), p.59.

67 Ibid., p.58.

68 Campbell Orr (ed.), *Women in the Victorian Art World*, p.40.

69 'The Art of Mr Issac Snowman', *Windsor Magazine*, 10 June 1904, p.39.

70 Devonshire Collection, Chatsworth House.

71 National Gallery of Scotland, Edinburgh.

72 Beckett and Cherry (eds), *The Edwardian Era*, p.81.

73 Steele, *Fashion and Eroticism*, p.217.

74 Jennifer Craik, *The Face of Fashion: Cultural Studies in Fashion* (London, Routledge, 1994), p.74.

75 *The Windsor Magazine, An Illustrated Monthly for Men and Women*, (London, Ward Lock, June 1904), p51.

76 Elizabeth Wilson, *Adorned in Dreams* (London, Virago, 1985), p.157.

77 *Windsor Magazine*, vol. xx, June–November 1904, p.217.

78 Camille Clifford in *The Prince of Pilsen*, 1904: Laver, *Edwardian Promenade*.

79   Osbert Sitwell, *The Scarlet Tree* (London, Macmillan, 1946).

80   The Women's Social and Political Union, formed in 1903 by Mrs Pankhurst in order to press for official party support for female enfranchisement, was ultimately central to the development of militant suffragism.

81   Rosemary Betterton, *Intimate Distance: Women, Artists and the Body* (London, Routledge, 1996), p.51.

82   Marina Warner, *Monuments and Maidens: The Allegory of the Female Form* (London, Weidenfield and Nicholson, 1985).

83   Lynda Nead, *The Female Nude: Art, Obscenity and Sexuality* (London, Routledge, 1992), p.157.

3 'Dehumanised Females and Amazonians': Fashion, Women's Magazines and the Female Body During the Great War, 1914–18

The outbreak of war on 4 August 1914 abruptly halted the ostentatious and excessive existence of the Edwardian ruling class. Dressing fashionably without recourse to wartime needs became highly contentious, and the female body in particular became a site for a range of tensions around class, nationality and gender. For women and men from different classes, war drew into even sharper relief those anxieties about feminine identities and women's roles which had surfaced during the escalating campaign for the vote just prior to 1914. With the onset of war, women experienced 'the collapse of those established, traditional distinctions between an '"economic" world of business and a private world of sentiment'.[1] For men, the war offered escape from the routines of social, economic and sexual responsibilities; it released them from the private sphere of home – the feminine world – and propelled them into 'the domain of the masculine, the army or navy, to the world of discipline, obedience, action'.[2] The spaces of war were clearly articulated as masculine, whereas women's spaces, particularly those of middle-class women, were perceived to be largely domestic. The highly public battles in which suffragists had engaged for the vote were put aside with the onset of war, although these campaigns provided an important background against which women's wartime activities were set. As Emmeline Pankhurst declared, 'it is obvious that even the most vigorous militancy of the WSPU is for the time being rendered less effective by contrast with the infinitely greater violence done in the present war'.[3] Meanwhile, in September 1914, in an article entitled 'They Also Serve', the *Home Chat* reader was exhorted,

> to keep a stiff upper lip and smiling front when things are going badly, to have a comforting word for the sad when we ourselves are almost in despair, to share our little with those who have less – these are gallant deeds which we can perform every day if we will...She will play her part unobtrusively

and as a matter of course. We can all be heroes in that state of life to which we are called. English women will no more be found wanting than English men in any trial of strength that comes.[4]

Women's prospects, sketched out in the pages of such magazines, were assertively traditional and, initially at least, saving within the home was to be their wartime role. As Gladys Owen, *Home Chat*'s cookery writer, put it in September 1914, 'economical housekeeping is a duty to every home in the land today'.[5] Women's duty was to support men in an unobtrusive fashion. Their 'gallant deeds' were to be found in the routines of everyday life rather than at the front. These routines, however, were to be disrupted as never before, as war affected not only those serving in France but also those left at home, who were employed in unprecedented numbers to help the war effort (Figure 3.1). From 1916, working- and middle-class women worked in many aspects of industry, commerce, banking and finance, the civil service, agriculture as part of the Land Army, and as bus conductors, ticket collectors and eventually bus drivers.[6] They also volunteered for various auxiliary organisations, such as the Voluntary Aid Detachment (VAD) and the Women's Army Auxiliary Corps (WAAC).[7]

The First World War presented women with an enormous challenge coping with new types of work outside the home, and for those who were married, of managing this alongside their traditional responsibilities of looking after the family during a time of shortages. In addition, they faced opposition

Figure 3.1: Women war workers at Darlington Railway Plant and Foundry, 1915.
Reproduced by permission of Darlington Borough Council.

from men in their new roles. Many women learned to take responsibility for all aspects of their lives and those of their families, gaining confidence and a different sense of self-worth which, as we will see, ultimately changed and challenged their sense of identity – particularly of who they were and who they might become. Defining and understanding women posed a new challenge for social commentators and for men alike. Pat Barker drew on this in 1991 in the first part of her First World War trilogy, *Regeneration*, when she discusses Second Lieutenant Billy Prior and Sarah, his munitions-worker girlfriend: 'He didn't know what to make of her, but then he was out of touch with women. They seemed to have changed so much during the war, to have expanded in all kinds of ways, whereas men over the same period had shrunk into a smaller and smaller space.' [8]

In discussing these changes, Susan Kingsley Kent has argued that historians have tended to reduce their assessment of the impact of war on women's lives to 'an exercise in measurement – of employment, wage levels, or rights'. [9] Instead, she proposes a more subtle analysis, one that takes account of shifts in identity, which are not so easily measured: 'these studies can tell us little about how ... [w]ar transformed the lives of men and women, their relationships with one another, and the cultural under-standings of gender and sexuality that informed their consciousness and sense of identity'. [10]

The fashionable female body is an exemplary site for exploring the construction of 'feminine' consciousness and identity. As Elizabeth Wilson has argued, fashion is 'obsessed with gender ... link[ing] the biological body to the social being, and public to private', and as a consequence it provides an important context for gauging the shifts in gender and feminine identities during wartime. [11] By looking at fashion and fashion imagery in women's magazines, particularly in the cheap popular weekly magazine *Home Chat*, but also in the more upper-class fashion journals such as *Coming Fashions, The Queen, the Lady's Newspaper and Court Chronicle* and *Vogue*, [12] it is possible to explore the 'cultural understandings of gender and sexuality'. [13]

Fashion – both in terms of the wearing of clothes and the representation of popular styles in magazines – was relatively accessible, popular and visual. It was an essential ingredient in the formula for a successful women's magazine in the period under discussion. Uniquely, it mapped out the social and cultural boundaries of the female body in the public and the private spheres during a period of great social upheaval. At work and at home the female body remained an aesthetic object, to be defined, refined and re-articulated, but between 1914 and 1918 a sense of urgency under-pinned the social and cultural definitions of the aestheticised, fashionable female body. Women were required to be feminine, but also serious and independent; they were to be 'womanly', but also to pull their weight in the war effort. Contradictory demands were made of women, and their bodies became a site where battle ensued.

Women's appearance was intrinsic to the war effort, but only certain types of feminine images were desirable: those based on an upper-middle-class ideal of womanhood as essentially decorative, idle and passive. Contradictory messages about the nature of femininity and female identity were increasingly evident in a range of representations of women found in art, design and literature during the First World War. However, it was in the plethora of cheap and expensive women's magazines prominently featuring fashion that these competing definitions of femininity were at their most accessible. As Margaret Beetham has argued: 'The fragmentation of the woman reader into different target groups was echoed in the cheap, as well as in the expensive journals, by the representations of the feminine self as fragmented, dispersed through the journal in its various constituent genres and in the advertisements'.[14] Such conflicting representations are evident in the pages of *Home Chat*, which avidly promoted new fashions and fashionable looks, and offered an infinite number of fashion tips. The frivolous and the highly practical co-existed, as in September 1914, when the *Home Chat* fashion editors, Camilla and the aristocratically styled Lady Betty advised on 'Easy to Make Fashions'. With little sense of contradiction, they wrote an article entitled 'Dress – Not Fashion' (10 October 1914), in which they argued, 'Nobody is thinking about fashion just now, but most of us will soon be thinking about a pretty blouse... a woman's duty is to try to make herself as nice as she can'.[15]

The contradictions between women's lives, their experiences of war, and the ways in which fashion and fashion imagery in magazines worked to represent these is at the centre of this discussion, but it is located within the larger context of modernity. In the first half of the twentieth century, the processes of modernity brought about a blurring of boundaries and categories; as Marshall Berman puts it,

> To be modern is to find ourselves in an environment that promises adventure, power, joy, growth, transformation of ourselves and the world – and, at the same time, that threatens to destroy everything we have, everything we know, everything we are...modernity can be said to unite all mankind. But it is a paradoxical unity, a unity of disunity; it pours us all into a maelstrom of perpetual disintegration and renewal, of struggle and contradiction, of ambiguity and anguish. To be modern is to be part of a universe in which, as Marx said, 'all that is solid melts into air'.[16]

In proposing the notion of an 'English' modernity, Alan O'Shea takes issue with Berman's concept of modernity as universal and globally undifferentiated.[17] He argues instead that Britain 'tended to move into the modern world looking backwards', and importantly for my arguments, he suggests that the English engagement with modernity, defined in terms of a 'structure of feeling', was uniquely 'English' and experienced differentially. Women's relationship to modernity was without question different to that of men, and it was also different for women from different social groups.

From the mid- to late nineteenth century there had existed a dissonance between women's lived experience and the predominantly patriarchal discourse of women's role as 'angel at home'.[18] Mica Nava has argued that in the early years of the twentieth century women's infiltration into all areas of social and cultural life was a defining moment of modernity. Most spectacular was the campaign for women's suffrage, which represented an unprecedented attack on the social mores of nineteenth-century patriarchy and which saw 'thousands of women from all social backgrounds [take] to the city streets in flamboyant, public and sometimes quite astonishingly violent protest against the injustice of disenfranchisement based on sexual difference'.[19] Embodied in the image of the New Woman, wearing a masculinised cropped jacket, straw boater and shortened skirt, young working women just prior to the First World War increasingly challenged the notion that women were the sole bastions of the 'traditional values' of home and family.

Fashion both fuelled and reacted to modernity, and as O'Shea argues it provided an important arena in which the working class as well as the middle and upper classes could engage with modernity: 'the working class did, early in the century, become major consumers of the new mass media and capitalised leisure activities – publishing, the cinema, the recording industry, radio, dancing, fashion'.[20]

Fashionable styles changed relatively quickly, and women's access to fashion information widened within the context of modernity.[21] Department stores, mail order, advertising, paper patterns and women's magazines were available to more women across the country. New styles from the fashion centres of London and Paris became widely diffused, and it was possible to see in magazines such as *Home Chat* the increasingly simplified rectilinear outlines which originated in the work of French couturier Paul Poiret (1879–1944).

Poiret provides an intriguing insight into the complex relationship between fashion and modernity during the First World War as his influence and popularity peaked in England as well as France. Between 1907 and 1918, he developed a distinctive style of dress which profoundly affected the overall look of fashion in England during this period. His designs, produced in the simultaneously reactionary and revolutionary atmosphere of *haute couture*, represented an intriguing example of a designer interpreting modernity and women's changing position within it. Designing for a wealthy, but heterogeneous, market that included actresses as well as aristocrats,

Poiret responded with some flamboyance to the artistic and cultural milieu of his day, to produce a complex synthesis of fashionable female images and to articulate a new ideal of female beauty. Generally the styles of Poiret represented a major shift in fashion design from the Edwardian era. The Poiret look was youthful, and the way in which the clothes covered the body was vastly different. Poiret's fashions were worn looser around the body, and designs such as the kimono coat from 1908 wrapped, rather than structured, the body. Especially striking were the colours which Poiret used – bold, vivid reds, purples, yellows and oranges, often dramatically combined with black. The overall outline was rectilinear, although occasionally the gown would be drawn tight under the breasts, but the natural waistline was almost completely disguised.[22] High-quality interpretations of the style dominated the fashion pages of upmarket magazines such as *Vogue*, but also it was increasingly apparent at the popular end of the market in magazines such as *Home Chat*. For practical everyday wear, a distinctive synthesis emerged which combined the simplicity of the Poiret look with the popular, ready-to-wear suit worn by the New Woman. According to Elizabeth Ewing, 'Poiret ... led the way to the modern tailored costume, which was a considerable liberation in fashion. With the new, comfortable, loose-waisted jacket and the straight off-the-ground skirt ... this rapidly became a classic.'[23]

The Poiret ideal woman was above all young and slim, with a hint of sexual innocence. Although he claimed to be a genius, it is clear that his ideas were firmly rooted in the various visual styles and social preoccupations of the day, and his designs, particularly those illustrated by the designer Paul Iribe in the published collection *Les Robes de Paul Poiret* in 1908, and those illustrated by Georges Lepape in *Les Choses de Paul Poiret* in 1911, represent a paradox with regard to femininity. In Poiret's autobiography, *My First Fifty Years* he claimed to have released women from the corset, 'in the name of Liberty'.[24] In fact, he re-designed the corset to enable a long, straight line to be created rather than the typical Edwardian S-bend. At the same time, in his use of the 'empire' line he looked back to the *directoire* styles popular at the end of the eighteenth century, and to the Pre-Raphaelite and Grecian styles adopted by dress reformers in England between 1870 and 1900.[25] Poiret was an eclectic designer who was familiar with new trends in fashion and design, particularly modernism, and this was apparent in his work. He had visited important exhibitions and met influential figures in the European art world. In 1911, he travelled to Vienna, where he met members of the Wiener Werkstätte, from whom he purchased large quantities of fabric, and he also travelled to Brussels to see the Palais Stoclet designed by Joseph Hoffmann.[26]

Modernity was a key element in Poiret's approach to the design of women's fashion, and in the fashion illustrations which promoted it. Heavily dependent on *haute couture* methods of production, the designs were nevertheless highly modern in appearance, in that they were radically simple and formally abstract. Pattern and decoration were crucial elements of his work, but they were deployed in an unorthodox manner to produce bold, radical designs. Poiret approached the use of colour, pattern and form in fashion design almost like a painter, by combining large, flattened shapes of strong colour with richly decorative, though abstracted, areas of pattern and ornament. Although the overall outline of his fashion design was often very simple, the completed garments were rarely so, and they depended on lavish, hand-printed silks, sumptuous velvets and heavy brocades, as well as delicate tulles.

The overall effect was highly contrived, making no attempt to follow the curves of the female body or to depict the 'natural' or the 'biological' body. In this respect, the artificiality of these designs firmly links Poiret to modernism and the concerns of his contemporaries in art, architecture and design. For many of these contemporaries, decoration and particularly pattern-making played an important role in the early years of modernist development, in removing art from the realm of the merely descriptive. Occupying a crucial role in the emergence of modernist art and design, but arguably effaced from later accounts of modernist practice and theory, the decorative and the domestic with which it became synonymous 'remain[ed] throughout the course of modernism a crucial site of anxiety and sub-version'.[27] In developing a language of fashion design which did not merely describe the shape of the body in a conventional manner, Poiret brought the female body into modernist discourse in a manner that was at odds with many of his artistic contemporaries. Although he shared their interest in abstraction and stylisation, as an *haute couturier* he designed for the 'social' body, whereas artists such as Henri Matisse continued to depict the 'idealised' female body of patriarchal discourse.

In this respect, Poiret's claim to be concerned for women's emancipation through dress was explicable, although problematic in the context of his frequent visual references to Orientalism. Such references were current within the wider culture of the time – for example Matisse had visited Morocco in 1911–12 and subsequently painted a number of odalisques, and the Russian ballets of Sergei Diaghilev had premiered in Paris in 1910 with *Schéhérazade*. This ballet had extraordinary sets and costumes by Léon Bakst which were highly decorative, richly patterned and evocative of Africa and the East. They were also highly sexualised and eroticised, but in very specific ways. Indeed what many of these oriental representations share is, as Griselda Pollock observed in her essay 'A Tale of Three Women' which deals with the work of Eduard Manet, a 'rhetorical combination of sex and servitude... in an economy that has slavery as its political unconscious, and sedimented in its social rituals and erotic fantasies'.[28] In this essay, Pollock shows how 'Africa – and its histories, complexly woven like a sign of the headwrap itself – is at the centre of modernity'.[29] Poiret clearly drew on this legacy in his important collections, as he incorporated garments such as harem pants, turbans and the hobble skirt which were richly and exotically decorated with luxurious gold and jewelled fabrics redolent of Africa and the East. By drawing on such a language to clothe and represent the female body, Poiret's designs evoked 'Europe's relations with the world it dominated through colonisation and exploited through slavery', and it is indicative of the paradoxical nature of his designs that he could simultaneously suggest a liberated female body and a 'colonised' one.[30]

Poiret's attempt to delineate and define female sexuality in such a way was also paradoxical, given that in France, England and the United States women had campaigned vigorously for the vote throughout the period in which he worked.[31] At a time when women were also highly visible on the streets, and as they engaged as never before in the world of business, industry and commerce, Poiret's fashionable ideal – intensely decorative with a half-glimpsed eroticism – positioned women half-way between the private space of the harem and the public space of the office. Poiret's designs, which are not easy to read in a singular way, were at once representative of the *ancien regime* and at the same time startlingly modern, marking 'a transition between the static styles of the nineteenth century and the modernism of Chanel'.[32] As an example, the Sack dress, designed in 1911, was extremely loose and casual. With its linear, unstructured outline, it draped and wrapped the body rather than controlling it. Languidly modelled by his wife Denise, there was nevertheless a hint of the 'other' in the sultry demeanour captured in the soft-focus photographic styling used to promote this design.

Poiret's designs effectively delineated the contradictions inherent in many representations of fashionably dressed women in this period, and they were clearly a response to the conflicting demands made of women at the cusp of modernity. Inevitably, these dichotomies between women's lived experiences and the visual representations of the female body through fashionable dress became more apparent as fashion images were more widely diffused in women's magazines, and as fashionable styles were within the grasp of larger sections of the population.

Characterising modernity as 'women's historical chance',[33] Rosi Braidotti has also argued that it represents 'the crisis of masculine identity in a hist-orical period when the gender system is being challenged and restructured'.[34] As a moment of restructuring, the First World War was without equal, and it can be persuasively argued that it was the decisive factor in delivering the vote (albeit with qualifications) to British women after half a century of campaigning.[35] It was the relative shift from a life dominated by patriarchal control and domestic responsibilities to one which brought women into contact with the outside world that most effectively ruptured gender identities during wartime. Women's wartime roles differed due to obvious factors such as class, age and marital status, but also due to the nature of the war, which saw a stark separation between the home and war fronts. Although uniformed servicemen were a familiar sight on city streets, and troops were highly mobile, most women did not directly confront the danger of war between 1914 and 1918.[36] They did, however, deal with the consequences of war; with the loss of their husbands, brothers, sons, friends and lovers, as well as with the physical damage and psychological scarring experienced by the survivors. At the same time, they learned to cope with the impact of war on the family, not just on their own children but also with the wider family who experienced loss and anxiety. For those women who served at the front, the experience was beyond comprehension, and from this they acquired 'a secret knowledge ... that transformed the consciousness, the senses, the very soul of the initiate, who was thereby ushered into a wholly different existence'.[37] As Vera Brittain put it, 'the war ... is too gigantic for the mind to grasp'.[38]

For those based at home, it was war work which was to transform their lives. Registration for war work had been an haphazard affair, only gaining a sense of purpose after 1915, when state intervention initiated the reorganisation of industry, and negotiations with employers and trade unions allowed the employment and training of women workers, particularly in the engineering and chemical trades.[39] By July 1916, the figures for women in the various metal and engineering industries (representing those industries producing munitions and equipment) had risen from 212,000 in July 1914 to 520,000.[40]

A direct result of new types of war work was that large numbers of young, single working-class women abandoned domestic service and sweated trades such as dressmaking for factory work.[41] Although domestic service was the largest employer of women at the time, the number going into service had been falling by the end of the nineteenth century, paradoxically as demand grew from the burgeoning middle class. Regarded by their families as respectable work, domestic service was deeply unpopular with young working-class girls.[42] Unhappy at the lack of freedom, many young women welcomed the opportunity to work in the new munitions factories, in which wages too could be significantly different.[43] As Diana Gittins wrote in 1982,

> The First World War provided a catalyst to change in all spheres of society. It precipitated the need for a more centralised government and for closer co-operation between the trade unions and the government. It was also the occasion for many women not only to experience greater independence, but also to be accepted (albeit reluctantly and temporarily) in occupations previously denied them.[44]

For married women from the working class with a home and children to manage, factory work offered better opportunities to supplement the family income than had existed before the war, when the possibility of combining work outside the home with caring for the family was very limited.[45] As Maud Pember Reeves stated, in 1913 roughly 50 per cent of adult working men in Britain earned 25 shillings or less each week.[46] To compensate for this, working-class married women had to be highly resourceful, managing woefully small amounts of money for rent, food and clothing. Often attempting to find paid work, they then faced extra costs for childcare, thus rendering the work uneconomical. At least wages for munitions work were capable of supporting some childcare, even if it was heavily dependent on the goodwill of neighbours and relatives.[47] Although there were many complaints about long hours, standing all day, and difficult journeys to work, according to Braybon and Summerfield, 'munitions work was undeniably fashionable'.[48]

Only 9 per cent of munition workers were from the middle or upper class, and many of those were supervisors or organisers. Middle-class women generally did not work. Their role was to manage the household, direct the servants, oversee the upbringing of the children and to maintain the home as a civilised retreat for the husband. However, there were increased opportunities for young, single middle-class women as jobs expanded in business as secretaries and typists, but also in the service sector, for example retailing, from the early years of the twentieth century. These jobs enabled women to gain some financial independence and the chance of a life outside the home. Wartime offered these young women greater opportunities as they took over white-collar jobs vacated by men – as Pugh has argued, 'Their families increasingly accepted the desirability, or even necessity, of their finding some means of supporting themselves after the war...[For women] a wider and more independent personal life often appeared to be the chief gain of the war years.'[49] Older married middle-class women with time on their hands and motivated by patriotism often volunteered for various public services and for the Land Army. Writing in *Women and Work* in 1945, Gertrude Williams reflected on the transformations to women's sense of identity brought by their involvement in the First World War: 'they had tasted the sweets of independence; they had widened their mental and social horizons...and they were determined not to give up lightly the control over their own lives that they gained by spending the money they earned for themselves'.[50]

Wartime experiences also jolted women's personal lives. Spending time with other women, they discussed more openly their marriages, their sexual feelings and attitudes. Married women's relationships with their husbands were sometimes questioned as they recognised men's complacency and their own lack of fulfilment. Sexuality was a particularly highly charged issue, and Susan Kingsley Kent argues that, following the First World War, discourses about female sexuality, which before the war had emphasized women's lack of sexual impulse, and even distaste for sexual intercourse, underwent modification to accommodate the political, social and economic requirements of the postwar period. The new accent on motherhood was accompanied by a growing emphasis on the importance of sexual activity, sexual pleasure, sexual compatibility between husband and wife.[51]

The anxieties underpinning these discourses of female sexuality frequently centred on the masculinisation of women's dress and the blurring of gender identities which arose from women wearing uniforms and factory clothes. This was particularly acute during the First World War, as such images clearly jarred against the dominant images of femininity previously evident. Such images also recalled to popular memory the pre-war struggle for women's suffrage and anti-suffrage feelings.[52] Writing in 1931, Caroline Playne remembered her perceptions of munitions workers:

> A short local train came in, drew up and disgorged itself, on the instant, a couple of hundred de-humanised females, Amazonian beings bereft of reason or feeling, judging by the set of their faces, bereft of all charm of appearance, clothed anyhow, skin stained a yellow-brown even to the roots of their dishevelled hair... Were these really women?[53]

Women's magazines and fashion magazines such as *Home Chat* and *Vogue* provided a crucial space in which representations of women were redefined. Margaret Beetham has argued that such magazines were characterised, by 'a radical heterogeneity'.[54] By this she means that they refused a single authorial voice, and as a consequence represented 'a fractured rather than rigidly coherent form'.[55] Drawing on the ideas of other cultural critics, Beetham discusses the proposition that the fragmentation of women's magazines makes them potentially subversive of men's cultural codes in a number of ways.[56] Mattelart, for example, identifies a 'feminine time', characterised by 'continuation, perpetuation, duration' rather than disruption and crisis.[57] The structure of women's magazines which deliver regular features and stories in a cyclical fashion, therefore, '[satisfies] the expectations of female subjective time'.[58] This format 'invites women to flip through, read in any order, omit some sections altogether', thereby enabling women to forestall the conventional narrative structure and to resist closure.[59] Ultimately Beetham rejects these ideas as essentialist and idealist, and argues instead that the format of women's magazines should be seen as a form of patriarchal regulation and capitalist expansion: 'Far from seeing serial forms as having been historically in tension with the dominant "masculine" values and power structures, then, I see them as consonant with and reinforcing those structures'.[60] By organising leisure within an increasingly industrialised and capitalist economy, Beetham identifies the periodical as a device for structuring time away from work and for regulating consumption.

Whilst accepting Beetham's argument about the regulatory and structural imperatives of women's magazines, it is also clear that during the First World War the identification and representation of gender identities remained highly problematic for the editors of women's magazines. There emerged a dissonance in some magazines, fundamentally between the depiction of women's changing roles – in effect, their lived experiences – and idealised, essentially patriarchal, definitions of femininity. This was manifested in a number of ways: in the factual reporting of what women were doing, in the fictional stories dealing with different aspects of women's lives, and in the visual representations of femininity in fashionable clothes, photography and illustration. In the array of titles for women's consumption, many of which were launched at the end of the nineteenth and the beginning of the twentieth centuries, including *Home Notes* (1894), *Home Chat*, *My Weekly* (1910) and *Woman's Weekly* (1911), the ideal of the gendered self as a fixed entity was increasingly questioned. By endlessly reiterating and rehearsing what it meant to be a woman and to be feminine through the magazine's characteristic formula, gender was, as Judith Butler has argued, 'structured by repeated acts'.[61] However, the First World War disrupted this repetition as never before, thus revealing the 'temporal and contingent' qualities of gender.[62] In this sense, wartime issues of magazines such as *Home Chat* and *Vogue* were simultaneously regulatory and liberatory.

In January 1914, seven months before the outbreak of war, *Home Chat* provided a distinctive formula for being a woman which was well established and familiar. For one penny, an array of advice and information was available, mainly concentrating on the traditional concerns of the home and the family, but with some references to jobs and careers.[63] In a feature called 'The Playbox', 'Aunt Molly' regaled both children and parents with stories, games and advice, whilst Gladys Owen provided cake recipes for tea parties and a step-by-step recipe guide for the reader.[64] Love and marriage figured prominently in both fiction and features and, significantly, women were given some practical advice in dealing with men. Weekly serial stories such as 'The Wrong Mr Right' by Berta Ruck, which told the story of Morwenna Beaugard, a typist earning £90 a year in an engineer's office who falls in love with the wrong man, provided examples of problematic relationships.[65] In June 1914, another feature asking 'Is any man easy to live with? A question that every woman sometimes asks of herself' elicited a surprisingly modern reply:

In a condition of society where one half [of] the world is economically dependent upon the other half, the dependent half takes orders with small protest. It has to. [However,] in the last twenty years women have become human beings. They have begun to reflect on their position. The fearful daughters of a past generation are to-day going their own way to work and to play.[66]

Changes in women's social and political position prior to the war clearly framed this assertion of their right 'to reflect on their position'. There was an implicit assumption throughout the magazine that, although romance and weddings were near the top of women's agendas, other issues were of interest to women, particularly so with the onset of war.[67] Along with subsequent historians, contemporary commentators detected a difference in women's consciousness during the First World War.[68] In *Home Chat* (3 July 1915), one writer, described as 'A Man o' the World', suggested 'Women are astounded at their own capacity – their own utility and value in the complex organism of ultra-modern life'.[69]

From September 1914, *Home Chat* assumed a new role: to map out a place for women within the conflict. The focus was initially on women's role on the domestic front, and in an article entitled 'Householders and the war', the editors asked, 'What ought we to do? What can we do to help our country, and to defend from want and distress those for whom we are responsible?'[70] The cover of the magazine, which were particularly important in visually representing its editorial content, shifted from images of romance and the young and fashionable to those dealing with war themes, as depicted in the first issue of October 1914, which under the headline 'Billeted. A story of war' depicted a billeted soldier playing the piano.[71] This particular image of a smart, educated young soldier contributing to a convivial evening at home was obviously designed to reassure those who harboured anxieties about having strangers billeted in their homes. Other articles dealt in a relatively factual way with aspects of wartime.[72] In the early years of the war, magazine covers showed women crocheting, and included articles such as 'Cook – on the war. On war-time manners' and 'How England "mothers" her army'.[73] At the same time there were already efforts to provide stories dealing with other aspects of life, which were designed to alleviate the gloom of war, such as the short story introduced with the headline 'Nothing to do with the war!', which gave a light-hearted account of 'Dolly of the dailies. The surprising adventures of a newspaper girl'.[74]

Alongside these, *Home Chat* ran features on the practical details of women's lives that such work threw into disarray, including childcare. Dr Truby-King, the magazine's health specialist, advised on 'feeding by the clock' for babies, and the advantages of the new creches were explained next to a photograph of the Woolwich Arsenal workers' creche.[75] Significantly, the magazine did not shy away from controversial subjects such as illegitimacy, war babies and unmarried mothers. The magazine's social observer, 'A Man o' the World', discussed the problems of war babies and illegitimacy in June

1915, pointing out that illegitimacy during wartime was not just an issue for the 'lower' classes.[76] Changing relationships between men and women were a regular feature of the magazine's content. A special issue in March 1915 had as its front cover an image of a young woman looking wistful under a headline 'Love and marriage in wartime'.[77] Implicit in such headlines was the question of how marriage could survive the impact of war, and it is interesting that there was recognition at the time that women's changing roles might affect their personal relationships at the end of the war.

Interest in romantic love and marriage was underpinned by an insistence on the importance of fashion and appearance in the pages of *Home Chat*, and although it is tempting to read this as evidence of the regulatory nature of such magazines, this also drew attention to the high level of concern around representations of the female body during wartime. Wartime sharpened and intensified the experience of modernity, and women's 'practical negotiation of . . . life and one's identity within a complex and fast-changing world' took on new meaning, as did their attempts to make sense of this visually through fashion.[78] *Home Chat* played a crucial part in articulating and delineating – on a weekly basis – new technologies and a vast array of consumer products for women, as well as pointing to new types of work and leisure, and personal relationships. Ostensibly about reaffirming women's traditional roles in making clothes and dressing up to meet social expectations, *Home Chat* also functioned to represent women's changing lifestyles, and although fashions could be both mundane and highly impractical, discussions of women's dress and appearance were firmly 'located' within the context of modernity. Dressing to tango, dressing for typing and dressing for munitions work were just different facets of the experience of modern life at war.

Fashion, as both social and cultural artefact and as representational process, was increasingly discursive during the period of the First World War, and it provided a highly charged space in which femininity, modernity and identity were negotiated. The fashionable female body in particular became an interface where different values and ideologies overlapped and competed, and definitions of the female body were firmly located in the gender uncertainties which accelerated and intensified. Often living away from home, young, single women in particular began to imagine themselves differently. By buying or making new clothes from their better wages, they used fashion to represent themselves. Even married and older women with a little more to spend could experience the pleasures of wearing new clothes. A magazine such as *Home Chat* tried to direct and inform women about fashion, but it sent out mixed messages. It attempted on the one hand to support women as they took on different responsibilities and as their approach to dress and appearance became more bold and questioning. But on the other hand it attempted to steer them towards images and roles which were not too contentious – practical, but at the same time feminine – often leading the magazine's editors and writers into uncertain territory.

Fashion, and the processes of representation that it involved, drew attention to key aspects of women's identity, particularly sexuality and gender, but also class, as it became less easy to read social status from dress. Land girls, for example, who were largely drawn from the working class, reputedly wore their breeches off duty, whereas wealthier women apparently made a fashion out of looking shabby, thus undermining the dress codes which had previously clearly delineated social status. Fashion allowed women to signal their new-found identities visually – even if it was only for the duration of war – by wearing uniforms or garments designed for work in the street for pleasure.[79]

There was a great deal of concern at the time that war was making women more 'masculine', as they took on modes of behaviour more typical of men – becoming independent and self-reliant, working outside the home, and managing their own finances. Their clothes became more practical in response to this, but such changes were often read at the time as masculine. As a report in the *Daily Mail* put it,

> The wartime business girl is to be seen any night out alone or with a friend in the moderate-priced restaurants in London. Formerly she would never have had her evening meal in town unless in the company of a man friend. But now with money and without men she is more and more beginning to dine out.[80]

It is telling that the reporter chooses to ignore the fact that some women had eaten out alone or with other women from the mid-nineteenth century, and that towards the close of the century department stores in particular provided facilities for women to dine alone whilst shopping.[81] Instead, the fact that women ate out alone was interpreted as a consequence of war.

Eating out became a necessity for some women when they were geographically isolated from their families, working as munitions workers and poorly served by cooking facilities in their temporary accommodation. With little time to spare between shifts, eating out and wearing their munitions clothes on the street was inevitable. This is evident in the poster designed by Septimus Scott, entitled 'These women are doing their bit. Learn to make munitions', which was produced to encourage women to take up munitions work (Figure 3.2). It depicts a young woman with her hair drawn back in a safety cap, pulling on her coat so as to rush off at the end of her shift. Wearing a plain, shortened calf-length skirt and blouse, this evocative wartime image highlights the sense of freedom experienced by the independent young munitions worker temporarily loose of familial ties. Such images suggest an entirely different world to the highly regulated life typical of domestic service endured by large numbers of working-class girls. Similarly, contemporary photographs of munitions workers, as well as those of VADS and WAACs, although less glamorous, show the clothed female body as being predominantly practical and informal. Calf-length loose dresses and uniforms, belted at the waist, brought an informality to women's dress that was unheard of a few years earlier. Clothes such as these reveal women as subjects rather than objects, engaged in active lives, outside the home and unconstrained by many of the social mores governing appropriate female behaviour. Such informality, integral to women's fashions both during and after the war, undercut the elaborate dress rituals which had previously epitomised upper-middle-class femininity. Recruitment posters and photographs of this type sent powerful messages to young women that they could be independent and could contribute to the war effort in a more dynamic way than knitting for the troops. Even so, as women's magazines show, fashion did not completely eschew the 'feminine' aspects of dress. Pretty fabrics, delicate bows and ribbons, glamorous makeup and brightly coloured scarves were combined to 'feminise' some of the more austere wartime looks. Nevertheless, women's fashion and fashionable images in magazines were sites of conflict, as women contested notions of 'ladylike' behaviour by dressing in ways which were less conventionally feminine.

Figure 3.2: 'These Women are doing their bit. Learn to Make Munitions'. Poster designed by Septimus Scott. Reproduced by permission of the Imperial War Museum, London.

In discussing *Home Chat* at the end of the nineteenth century, Beetham writes:

> *Home Chat* assumed that physical appearance was central to femininity and that in this respect at least women were not born but made and made themselves. Even 'the plain girl' could make herself 'as popular and charming as her Beautiful Sister'. Central to that making was 'fashion' which was explicitly linked to the ideal of the Lady.[82]

The ideal of being a 'lady' was crucial in defining femininity in magazines such as *Home Chat*, and during wartime as class distinctions as well as gender relations were disrupted, such an ideal was especially important. Many working-class women worked in close proximity to women from the middle and upper classes; however, there were key differences in approach to dress and fashion, as well as to ladylike behaviour. Whereas middle- and upper-class women could enjoy the privilege of dressing up to their 'normal' social position and dressing down to demonstrate their patriotism and commitment to the war effort (by wearing uniform or shabby work clothes on the streets), the better-off working- and the lower-middle-class readership of *Home Chat* was generally eager to use new earnings whenever possible to buy better, smarter and more fashionable clothes. Magazines such as *Home Chat* fulfilled a crucial role in guiding and directing the purchasing capacity of these new consumers of fashionable clothes.

The *Home Chat* reader was advised on dress by Camilla and Lady Betty. Shortly after war was declared, they responded with an article for 'All easy to make', 'for those who haven't made their own clothes before, but now feel a duty to do so. Still chic and fashionable though, but with a little more stress on practicality'.[83] This theme of wartime practicalities was evident throughout the pages of *Home Chat*, although the editors found the lure of fashion for its own sake hard to resist. Whereas one issue might suggest that 'The reign of fashion is over for many and many a long day...The aim of fashion writers and designers to-day is to show how plainly other people are dressing, not how elaborately',[84] another issue dictated that 'the narrow skirt is a thing of the past, and the new one measures sometimes as much as six yards around the hem'.[85] These apparent contradictions led to the emergence of a number of representations of appropriate fashionable looks for women, as those clad in breeches and short skirts appeared in the same issues as those wearing clothes in the latest fashion. These were rather elongated and simplified at the outset of war, but by 1916 a clearly defined waistline was discernible (Figures 3.3 and 3.4). According to Camilla and Lady Betty, writing in 1916, 'women are to present a more fluffy, feminine appearance than has been the case for some long while. The trend in favour of a less masculine style in dress is unmistakable'.[86] Accompanying this 'fluffy femininity' was, however, a marked casualness which differentiated women's fashions from those of ten years earlier, and which suggests a response to the more recent experiences of wearing clothes for wartime work. The highly corseted outline of the Edwardian era was replaced by a looser, less structured look which nonetheless required the aid of corsets. Softly gathered blouses with wide, unstarched collars were tucked into narrow skirts which draped and ruched at the waist, rather than being panelled and gored. Feminised ties were often worn around the neck, and decolletage was open and informal. The 'easy-to-make' patterns included in *Home Chat* allowed women a good deal of flexibility to mix items of fashion as they desired, and recommended fabrics often included those, like cotton, that were hard-wearing and practical. Although the patterns were quite complex and could be difficult to follow, most women had some dressmaking skills acquired as young girls, and improved upon as the demands of

Figure 3.3: 'All Easy to Make', *Home Chat*, 5 September 1914.
Reproduced by permission of the British Library.

Figure 3.4: 'Summer frocks', *Home Chat*, 20 May 1916.
Reproduced by permission of the British Library.

family life required. For those with a little more money, a visit to the home of a local dressmaker and the purchase of materials from the nearby draper would be sufficient to acquire a moderately priced new outfit. Drapers shops dominated small towns and cities throughout Britain, and although they tended not to lead the way in stylistic innovation, such knowledge could be gained from the magazines and from department stores. Through such mechanisms, the look of high fashion reached a wider audience.

The fashion advice in *Home Chat* was supported by the inclusion of very practical information about all aspects of women's beauty and grooming. In an article entitled 'What should a typist wear?', those confused about office dress codes were advised to wear 'a plainly-made serge costume. Nothing about it to date. Just plain with a stock collar and tie...And if a girl must have some sort of colour about her outdoor attire she could easily introduce it in wings on her hat.'[87] The unmistakable uniform of the New Woman was described as the obvious solution to the problems facing working women. It was practical and smart, but importantly it also functioned as a symbol of emancipation and modernity. Generally, the magazine aimed to balance the traditional and the modern, both in jobs and leisure, and for those intent on the latter, in the previous week's issue the fashion editor had directed them to the latest styles:

> Everyone is mad about the tango, and dresses are made specially for it. The short, slit, draped Liberty or velvet skirt, with a full tunic dropping lower behind than in front, is the most graceful thing so far, otherwise the effect of the body in movement is decidedly ungraceful. Very light and brilliant colours can be worn at a tango tea in Paris, and there is a certain tomato red which is specially named 'tango' that one sees a great deal.[88]

The dipped hem-line of the dance dress (Figure 3.4) and the smart practicality of the serge costume and blouse (Figure 3.3) epitomised different but related facets of modernity. Both were glamorous and chic, but a sense of movement, spectacle and performance influenced the diaphanous bodices, panniered skirts and slit or uneven hemlines of the dance dress. Dancing the tango required a type of physical flamboyance and lack of restraint which was at odds with the behaviour of the pre-war generation. Equally at odds, but for different reasons, was the remarkably minimal 'tailor-made' suit which epitomised the young, working woman in a man's world, albeit a 'feminised' and glamorised one. This latter image evoked most forcefully the inroads that women were making into the world of work, a process exacerbated by wartime needs. A number of 'femininities' co-existed then within women's wardrobes and with the aid of *Home Chat* paper patterns, women could move relatively seamlessly from one identity to the other in the peculiar circumstances that existed during wartime. The ultra-'femininity' evoked by these wide, flowing dance skirts was seemingly at odds with women's increasing confidence outside the home, yet they were part of a wardrobe which might also include uniforms, munitions clothes and masculine forms of work clothes.

As the war continued, *Home Chat* included articles that outlined suitable clothes for munitions and other types of war work. In 'Dress for war workers', photographs showed young women workers wearing bloomers and skirts that were just below the knee, alongside an article which declared: 'It looks as if war-time work would bring about something of a revolution in women's workday attire...There is no doubt about it that you are HANDICAPPED if you go haymaking or harvesting or gardening or feeding the pigs in an ordinary skirt.'[89]

The photographs accompanying this piece showed women wearing skirts which were just below the knee for gardening, and gaiters, a long linen coat and Panama hat for haymaking. Another article in the same month discussed the dress of the 'Lady postmen', who looked 'very neat and business-like...in their plain skirts and blouses, with their bags slung over their shoulder'.[90] In both articles, the discussion of suitable dress for war work was couched in the language of fashion, in order to emphasise women's duty to remain at all times within the bounds of what was considered feminine. The photographs of the women gardening and haymaking were accompanied with credits which declared 'Fashions for gardening' and 'Fashions for hay-making', whereas the garments were clearly intended as practical work clothes. This particular article examined the background to reformed dress prior to the war, and it reminded its readers of the 'hideous and ridiculous' bloomers which were now, in the special conditions of wartime, described as practical and appropriate items of dress.[91] A few years earlier, bloomers had been tolerated for sport, but, as the writer in *Home Chat* made clear, in the public mind they were associated with the suffrage movement.

Representations of reformed styles of work dress drew on a range of different visual codes than those used in fashion features. Work dress was mod-elled by women doing particular jobs: the parcels lady wore a shortened skirt and three-quarter coat on her bicycle; the agricultural worker wore trousers, a shirt and straw hat as she dug in a field; and the Southampton tramway conductors wore 'short sensible skirts' just below the knee as they ran up and down the high steps of the tram.[92] The static, languidly posed images adopted to represent the latest fashions were eschewed for photographs of women in the process of working, thus emphasising the practicality of their clothes.

Permeating the writings on fashion and dress in *Home Chat* was an attempt to provide some sort of rationale for these highly contradictory messages about the nature of femininity, which directly addressed the reader's expectations and prejudices. An article from 1916, entitled 'How the girl of the period faces war' and liberally illustrated with images of women wearing breeches and uniforms, revealed the difficulties which this posed (Figure 3.5). Regretting 'such an old head on young shoulders', the writer admitted that the modern girl is 'self-willed and full of assurance...and absolutely determined to get her own way'. At the same time, acknowledging the country's dependence on 'these fearless young women', now an important resource, the writer added ruefully, 'well we made her ourselves. When she was in the nursery we were greatly allured by the dogma of feminine emancipation, and preached the rights of individualism for every creature.'[93]

The attempt to reconcile apparently contradictory expectations of women's wartime roles was also obvious on the magazine's front cover. In two consecutive months in 1916 (18 March and 15 April), the cover of *Home Chat* showed women in positions of responsibility. On the first, two women medical students were shown doing their rounds. Accompanying this

Figure 3.5: Women farm workers wearing breeches, *Home Chat*, 18 March 1916.
Reproduced by permission of the British Library.

photograph was a credit which declared, 'Owing to the great shortage of doctors the women medical students are in great demand at the hospitals, where they are doing excellent work for the wounded'.[94] Yet contrasting with this, just a few weeks later, the front cover for 29 April 1916 depicted a wedding image of a woman gazing devotedly at a man. Clearly the interplay between such text and photography reveals the difficulties faced by the editors and writers of *Home Chat* in trying to negotiate an acceptable path during such uncertain times. The reality for a large section of the magazines' readership was that war produced unconventional lives, and fashion and dress was just one of a number of things that had to adapt. Women were changing in ways that were inconceivable to the pre-war generation, and representations of the fashionable female body in *Home Chat* undoubtedly contributed to this.

Whereas *Home Chat* specifically addressed the war and the different ways in which it influenced women's lives across a fairly wide social spectrum, fashion magazines such as *Coming Fashions, The Queen, the Lady's Newspaper and Court Chronicle*[95] and *Vogue* remained largely unaffected. Instead, they continued to reaffirm particular class interests and to restate the social mores of the upper and upper-middle classes. Unlike *Home Chat*, which addressed a larger audience, *The Queen*, for example, typically approached the war in a more conventional manner by focusing on abstract concepts such as King and Queen, the army and the country, rather than the harsher details of wartime cooking, childcare and personal relationships. During 1916 and 1917, as *Home Chat* produced editorial, features and visual images that dealt with the war on a weekly basis, a magazine such as *Coming Fashions*, costing 6d and subtitled *La Mode de Demain*, concerned itself entirely with the nuances of high fashion. Advertisements, such as those for winter sales at Whiteley's and Swan & Edgar, and furniture at Shoolbred's co-existed with lengthy features explaining the details of the very latest French and English blouses, hats and frocks. A vaguely military style could be seen in some of the designs in *Coming Fashions*, revealing a minimal nod to wartime conditions, but couched in the language of modernity and practicality, rather than of wartime necessities. In contrast, *The Queen* displayed a fairly conventional message of patriotism and duty. It included features on 'The country and the war', 'The Queen's message to the troops' and 'Young women wanted for the Land Volunteer Force'.[96] Nevertheless, women's appearance was still paramount, and as well as illustrating the Paris fashions of Lanvin, Worth and Jenny, the magazine proffered advice from Helena Rubenstein on, 'The rejuvenation of war-worn faces'. Makeup was one of a number of devices utilised in order to construct an image of normality in the context of wartime pressures, and Helena Rubenstein advertised in a similar manner in other magazines at the time. One such advert (15 September 1915) advised *Vogue* readers,

> The period for economy nowadays is very real... At the same time it must not be forgotten that one may be 'penny wise and pound foolish'... it is obvious that the strain of the War is causing many women to lose their good looks, which... is most undesirable from the professional or social point of view.[97]

Beauty was a primary concern of these relatively select fashion magazines, and in their pages particular notions of female beauty were constructed and reinforced. These ideals were drawn from a number of sources, including paintings, fashion illustration, photography and early cinema. A photographic portrait of Viscountess Errington in *Vogue* in early February 1917 encapsulated a distinctive, class-specific type of femininity, one which was pale, refined and delicate, essentially passive and above all meant to be admired (Figure 3.6). This particular image of large doleful eyes, long elegant neck, and flowing hair parted in the middle and drawn up at the nape refers back to Pre-Raphaelite iconography. This was reinforced by the 'empire-line' gown that effectively obscured the natural waistline and flattened the breasts, and by the informality of the draped shoulder-line. This fragile and girl-like image drew on the particular language of fashion developed by Poiret, and it marked a surprising contrast with the mature and maternal Edwardian female figures of just ten years earlier.

Significantly, Viscountess Errington symbolised an ideal of female beauty which was not merely passive, unquestioning and sexually innocent, but also racially pure. Within a contemporary context of social engineering and eugenics which crossed the political spectrum (and included some feminists),

Figure 3.6: Viscountess Errington, *Vogue*, early February 1917.
Reproduced by permission of the British Library.

the delicacy, paleness and refinement of such female images served as an effective reminder of the threat to the nation which the war exacerbated.[98] As Vron Ware put it, 'when theories of race and eugenics were being used to bolster the concept of the innate superiority of the white race above all others, English women were seen as the "conduits of the essence of the race"'.[99] Particularly powerful 'conduits' were photographic portraits of bourgeois white women who symbolised racial and moral purity. As Richard Dyer and others have argued, specific photographic devices were used to create a sense of lightness and translucency in such portraits.[100] These portraits were often softly focused to suggest immateriality, as opposed to 'the brutal, scrutinising quality of criminal, medical, eugenic and much ethnographic photography'.[101] These images of upper-class aristocratic women were literally symbols of light, and during the First World War such lightness contrasted with the darkness of the enemy. Dyer discusses the importance of early cinema, in particular stars such as Lillian Gish and Mary Pickford, who, in films such as *Hearts of the World* (directed by D.W. Griffith in 1918), constructed 'the glow of white women, contrasted ... with a dark masculine desire that, under the pressure of war propaganda, would also have been felt as racially other'.[102]

The photograph of Viscountess Errington drew on codes of representation which were characteristic of portraiture at that time, particularly by concentrating on the head, to reveal the 'inner being', and the hands, to suggest delicacy and refinement. As Suren Lalvani has argued, 'The arrangements of heads and hands in nineteenth-century bourgeois portraiture are traversed by a physiognomic intention: the need to convey the notion of manifest destiny central to bourgeois ideology; that the world may be civilised by the appropriate combination of head and hand'.[103] Articulating notions of racial purity and class distinction, such images were immensely significant as Britain not only engaged in an herculean struggle with Germany in Europe, but also defended its colonial interests from the stirrings of nationalism, particularly in India, but also in Egypt and East Africa.[104]

As a category, the 'feminine' was at the intersection of a range of discourses, and inevitably representations of femininity in *Vogue* highlighted this, although differently to *Home Chat*. Discontinuities were discernible in *Vogue* as social, political and economic ideologies were exposed by the magazine's formulaic structure. In contrast to *Home Chat*, *Vogue* was invested with a greater commitment to maintaining the status quo with regard to class identities, and *haute couture* was part of the armoury deployed to articulate a distinctive, class-specific 'high femininity'. New and traditional forms of visual representation were also marshalled for these purposes, and both the well-established photographic genre of portraiture and the new forms of fashion illustration which epitomised modernity were adopted for this.

As the Viscountess Errington portrait makes evident, photographic portraiture drew on recognisably bourgeois visual codes. At the same time, although these aristocrats had lifestyles which were far removed from the masses, photography rendered them tangible at least. In contrast, fashion illustration was patently 'artificial', and unlike photography it had no purchase on what was 'real', it was thus the ideal medium for the creation of a particular type of femininity which connected in important ways with the modernity of contemporary life. This new form of fashion illustration became yet another arena for mapping out the contradictions inherent in the range of feminine identities evident during the First World War. Although Viscountess Errington wore a gown which pointed directly to the modernity of Poiret's designs, the use of the specific photographic device of portraiture conjured up established codes and meanings which served to reinforce the status quo. However, in the sections of the magazine devoted to *haute couture*, which aimed to inform and survey the fashion scene, the images of women were ultra modern, and they were directly influenced by the work of Poiret, and the illustrators of his work, particularly Iribe and Lepape.

The impact of Poiret and his contemporaries on fashion in France and England was immense, and he directly inspired the fashionable images found in English *Vogue* during the years of the First World War. *Vogue*'s illustrations from this period captured perfectly the modernity of Poiret's designs, yet they also suggest the patriarchal and racial framework within which his ideas emerged. The Christmas cover of *Vogue* of 1916 was a flamboyant design illustrated in a style which was entirely typical of Poiret. A young woman wearing a large three-quarter-length flared coat edged with white fur over harem or cossack trousers edged with the same fur and tucked into side-laced boots dominated the cover (Figure 3.7). The illustration depicted the coat at the moment of being swung and wrapped around the model, giving a sense of movement and informality. Wearing a white fur hat pulled down over the face, the model's eyes looked downwards in a demure gesture. The illustrative style was highly simplified and stylised, using a few bold lines combined with large flat areas of colour. The overall sense of the image is of modernity, although the female image is both modern and conservative. The woman's face and body is fragile and delicate, and although she is captured informally, mid-movement, the modernity of the moment is undermined by her downward, almost coy gaze. Here is a girl-woman – vulnerable and delicate – curiously pre-sexual, although the suggestion of 'otherness', achieved as much by the elements of fashion design (white fur and exotic harem trousers) as by the illustrative style, adds a sexual frisson to the image. It connects in some ways with those early cinematic images of the innocent heroine cringing from unwanted male advances, as described by Dyer, 'the light catches her wide eyes and the whiteness of her face is emphasised by the contrast with the darkness of the wall'.[105]

Figure 3.7: Front cover of English *Vogue*, Christmas 1916.
Reproduced by permission of Condé Nast Publications Ltd.

Fragile, child-like models dominated the fashion pages of *Vogue* during this period. With pale faces, sweetheart red lips, and wearing Poiret-style outfits, a very youthful, insubstantial feminine ideal could be seen in page after page of *Vogue* illustrations. The contrast with the Edwardian ideal of a few years earlier was particularly marked. Ostensibly images of modernity, these Poiret-influenced fashion designs and illustrations signalled vulnerability, and it was significant that as patriarchal ties loosened during wartime, the imposingly mature and sexually confident *fin de siècle* woman was replaced, paradoxically, by this mere slip of a girl.

War impinged only rarely on the regular features in *Vogue*, and it barely registered as a serious cause for concern in the fashion pages. Although the issue of *Vogue* from early February 1918 included a discussion of the important role of lady supervisors in the munitions factories, a more typical feature was the illustrated fashion special from September 1916.[106] This depicted fashion models clearly in the Poiret mode, with pale, child-like features accentuated by strikingly dark lips and eyes, under a title announcing 'When Florence Walton was not dancing in Paris in aid of the American ambulance, she found time to acquire these Doeuillet and Callot suits'.[107] These particular illustrations show models wearing a variety of turbans and large-brimmed hats which shadowed the face, combined with loose, relatively unstructured dresses and winter coats which fell from under the breasts or from the shoulder. All the illustrations were set against bare white backgrounds to highlight the modernity of the designs.

These high-fashion images dominated representations of femininity in *Vogue*. However, the commercial exigencies of *Vogue*, newly launched in English in 1916, brought other representations which were particularly evident in its advertising and in some of its features. One of *Vogue*'s functions was to outline the social calendars and diaries of the English aristocracy and to advise on forthcoming weddings, marriages and appearances at court. However, as a commercial venture selling advertising and promoting particular designers, department stores and products, it had to appeal to a larger market than that which it instinctively sought to represent. Clear evidence of this in *Vogue* is the promotion of paper patterns which enabled the less wealthy to acquire 'Paris models'. Paper patterns illustrated in the September 1916 issue utilised a similar illustrative technique to that found on the main fashion pages. These cost 3–4 shillings and, although they were an important device in the diffusion of Paris *couture* designs into the wider market, they were complex and required professional interpretation.[108]

Advertising in *Vogue* also had to address a different, wider and less well-off market. Here images of the well-heeled 'county set' wearing 'Dexters' weatherproofs co-existed with advertisements for Helena Rubenstein, department stores such as Selfridges, and a variety of restorative and domestic products. Evident from such advertising was the dilemma faced by *Vogue* as it attempted to find a niche with the upper classes, but at the same time to tap into the increasingly affluent middle-class market for fashionable clothes and beauty products.

Indeed, one can see that during wartime, the weekly *Home Chat* (priced at 1d) was much better poised than the fortnightly and more expensively priced *Vogue* (at 1 shilling) to engage with the complexity of women's wartime lives. From a formal, visual standpoint, *Home Chat* appeared more conservative, whereas *Vogue* was much more modern in appearance. Due to the needs of its expanding lower-middle-class readership, *Home Chat* offered a lively formula of articles which depicted the range of experiences and ambitions of women. It revealed the complexities and the discontinuities in women's lives during wartime by examining a number of aspects of their experience, including home and work, love and sex, fashion and appearance, as well as their attitudes to war and their roles in it. In contrast, due to its structural relationship to the world of *haute couture*, *Vogue* was compelled to focus on the traditional upper and upper-middle classes, who had the money to buy *couture* garments, even though it maintained at least half an eye on the larger market. However, the fashionable looks articulated in the pages of *Vogue* were highly paradoxical. Ostensibly pointing to a more liberated look, the designs which had been inspired by Poiret had other meanings which located women in a position of relative powerlessness within patriarchy. At the same time, the photographic portraits of aristocratic, fashionable women which proliferated in the pages of *Vogue* operated ideologically to construct the notion of racial and class purity at a time of perceived threats to national identity and social status.

Arguably it was in the pages of *Home Chat*, with its wide, varied readership requiring more diverse and practical responses to women's needs during wartime, that there emerged a 'dissonance' between women's 'lived experiences' and the visual representations of femininity in fashion. This could be acute in particular issues of the magazine, as images of modernity which showed women working in the munitions factories, doing jobs previously done by men, or dominating areas of work such as office work or retailing were often coupled with discussions of fashion and appearance which might refer back to a previous femininity, but also forward to their new needs as workers. Inevitably these images sat uneasily alongside other visual material which represented romantic love, the perfect wedding and the ideal home. In such representations it is clear that women's fashion and appearance constituted a 'feminised' arena during wartime in which gender identities were contested. The disruption of apparently 'stable' gender identities was more marked in a magazine such as *Home Chat* than in the upmarket *Vogue*. Indeed, although dominant codes of representations of femininity were undermined in *Vogue*, this occurred primarily at the formal level, in the deployment of a distinctive illustrative style, and its engagement with modernity was discernible in the modernism of its fashion illustrations and photography rather than in its content. Images of modernity in *Vogue*, which ultimately derived from the aesthetic concerns of Poiret rather than wartime exigencies, were harbingers of patriarchy as much as modernity.

NOTES ON CHAPTER 3

1   Susan Kingsley Kent, *Making Peace: The Reconstruction of Gender in Interwar Britain* (Princeton, Princeton University Press, 1993), p.14.

2   Kingsley Kent, *Making Peace*, pp.12–3.

3   Martin Pugh, *Women and The Women's Movement in Britain 1914–1959* (London, Macmillan, 1992), p.7.

4   'They Also Serve', *Home Chat*, LXXVIII/1016 (5 September 1914), p.436.

5   'How I Economise', *Home Chat*, LXXVIII/1016 (5 September 1914), p.459.

6   In July 1914 there were 3,276,000 women in industry, by April 1918 there were 4,808,000 – an increase of over 1.5 million. The biggest increase was in the chemical and engineering trades, which included munitions. See Gail Braybon and Penny Summerfield, *Out of the Cage: Women's Experiences in Two World Wars* (London, Pandora, 1987), pp.38–9.

7   By November 1918, there were 40,000 in these services, largely in the VADs and WAACs. See Braybon and Summerfield, *Out of the Cage*, p.44.

8   Pat Barker, *Regeneration* (London, Viking, 1991), p.90.

9   Kingsley Kent, *Making Peace*, p.3.

10   Ibid.

11   Elizabeth Wilson, *Adorned in Dreams* (London, Virago, 1985), pp.2, 117.

12   See in particular *Home Chat* (1895–1956), a cheap popular weekly journal for the home which cost one penny in 1914; in the glossier magazines, such as *Coming Fashions* (1913–34), which cost sixpence in 1917, *The Queen*, the *Lady's Newspaper and Court Chronicle* (1861–1970), costing one shilling in 1918, as well as *Vogue* (1916–), at that time the latest upmarket magazine.

13   For further information on women's magazines in addition to Beetham, cited above, see Ros Ballaster et al. (eds), *Women's Worlds: Ideology, Femininity and the Woman's Magazine* (London, Macmillan, 1991); Marjorie Ferguson, *Forever Feminine: Women's Magazines and the Cult of Femininity* (London, Heinemann, 1983); Ellen McCraken, *Decoding Women's Magazines* (Basingstoke, Macmillan, 1993); Cynthia White, *Women's Magazines, 1693–1968* (London, Michael Joseph, 1970); Janice Winship, *Inside Women's Magazines* (London, Pandora, 1987).

14   Beetham, *A Magazine of Her Own*, p.191.

15 'Easy to Make Fashions', *Home Chat*, LXXVIII/1016 (5 September 1914), pp.443-4; 'Dress Not Fashion', *Home Chat*, LXXIX/1021 (10 October 1914), p.53.

16 Marshall Berman, *All That is Solid Melts Into Air: The Experience of Modernity* (London, Verso, 1985), p.15.

17 Alan O'Shea, 'English Subjects of Modernity', in Mica Nava and Alan O'Shea, *Modern Times: Reflections on a Century of English Modernity* (London, Routledge, 1996), pp.8, 31.

18 See, for example, Lynne Walker, 'Vistas of Pleasure: Women Consumers of Urban Space in the West End of London 1850–1900', in Campbell Orr, *Women in the Victorian Art World*; Mica Nava, 'Modernity's Disavowal: Women, the City and the Department Store', in Nava and O'Shea, *Modern Times*.

19 Nava and O'Shea, *Modern Times*, p.45.

20 O'Shea, 'English Subjects of Modernity', in Nava and O'Shea, *Modern Times*, p.29.

21 The best discussion of this remains, in my view, Wilson, *Adorned in Dreams*.

22 A notable and infamous exception to this is the hobble skirt which was narrow around the hem thus greatly restricting movement. Also such items as the lampshade tunic were highly impractical. For more details see Alice Mackerell, *Paul Poiret* (London, Batsford, 1990).

23 Elizabeth Ewing, *History of 20th Century Fashion* (London, Batsford, n.d.), p.66.

24 Paul Poiret, *My First Fifty Years* (London, Gollancz, 1934).

25 The taste for classical idioms was pervasive in all aspects of the decorative arts in France in the 1910s, as French designers sought for a new style of design that would guarantee French export markets and protect home markets from foreign competition. To a certain extent it was imperative to draw upon the well-established traditions of French craftsmanship and quality in the decorative arts, and for this purpose the Rococo style and the First and Second Empire styles were re-worked. In an illustration such as 'La tunique Josæphine', found in Paul Iribe's *Les robes de Paul Poiret*, the classical influence was most apparent. The design consisted of a long, high-waisted dress in white satin with a black tulle tunic edged with gold, classically-inspired braid. In the background are a number of objects in the neo-classical style, including a sideboard and a sculpture.

26 See *Addressing the Century: 100 Years of Art and Fashion* (London, Hayward Gallery, 1998), p.10. The formal devices used by the Wiener Werkstätte designers, such as small repetitive, abstract and geometric patterns, appeared in Poiret's designs shortly after this date.

27 Christopher Reed, *Not at Home: The Suppression of Domesticity in Modern Art and Architecture* (London, Thames and Hudson, 1996), p.16.

28 Pollock, *Differencing the Canon*, p.294.

29 Ibid.

30   Ibid.

31   In England, women gained the vote with restrictions in 1918, following high-profile suffrage campaigns, in the USA women gained the vote in 1920, and although it was not until 1945 that French women gained the vote, a bill failed in the French senate in 1922 following intense campaigning.

32   Wilson, *Adorned in Dreams*, p.139.

33   Rosi Braidotti, *Nomadic Subjects: Embodiment and Sexual Difference in Contemporary Feminist Theory* (New York, Columbia University Press, 1994), p.242.

34   Ibid., p.239.

35   Lisa Tickner, *The Spectacle of Women: Imagery of the Suffrage Campaign 1907–14* (London, Chatto & Windus, 1987), p.236.

36   In contrast to the Second World War, in which war was 'at the doorstep', and large numbers of women were killed during the blitz. Of 130,000 civilians killed during the Blitz, 63,000 were women. Pugh, *Women and The Women's Movement in Britain 1914–1959*, p.264.

37   Kingsley Kent, *Making Peace*, p.52.

38   Quoted by Kingsley Kent, *Making Peace* (from Vera Brittain's *War Diary*, October 1915), p.53.

39   This was undertaken by Lloyd George after he gained office in May 1915. A voluntary arrangement was negotiated, known as the Treasury Agreement, which enabled unskilled women to take over some skilled men's jobs, or aspects of them.

40   Arthur Marwick, *Women at War 1914–1918* (London, Fontana, 1977), p.73. See also George A. Wade, 'Open Doors for Women Workers: Wonderful Changes', *Home Chat*, LXXXI/1051, p.227.

41   At the start of war, the numbers of women in domestic service stood at 1,658,000, but by 1918 the number was 1,258,000. Pugh, *Women and The Women's Movement in Britain 1914–1959*, pp.19–20.

42   Braybon and Summerfield, *Out of the Cage*, p.16.

43   Whereas a housemaid could earn a paltry 5 shillings a week, a munitions worker could earn £3 a week (possibly £4 with overtime): ibid., p.58.

44   Diana Gittins, *Fair Sex: Family Size and Structure 1900–1939* (London, Hutchinson, 1982), p.34.

45   Except in a few areas of the Midlands and the North of England (the potteries and the Lancashire cotton mills were examples), working-class women were expected to stop work after marriage. However, those in desperate circumstances worked at home, taking in sewing or washing.

46   Maud Pember Reeves, *Round About A Pound A Week* (London, Virago, 1994), p.213.

47   Braybon and Summerfield, *Out of the Cage*, pp.105–7, for a discussion of childcare.

48   Braybon and Summerfield, *Out of the Cage*, p.62.

49 Pugh, *Women and The Women's Movement in Britain 1914–1959*, p.22.

50 Gertrude Williams, *The New Democracy: Women and Work* (London, Nicholson & Watson, 1945), p.57.

51 Kingsley Kent, *Making Peace*, p.108.

52 See Jenny Gould, 'Women's Military Services in First World War Britain', in Margaret Randolph Higonnet and Jane Jenson (eds), *Behind the Lines: Gender and the Two World Wars* (New York, Yale University Press, 1987).

53 Cited in Kingsley Kent, *Making Peace*, p.37.

54 Beetham, *A Magazine of Her Own*, p.12.

55 Ibid.

56 She cites the writings of Michele Mattelart, such as *Women Media Crisis: Femininity and Disorder* (London, Comedia, 1986); see pp.15–6.

57 Ibid., p.15.

58 Ibid., p.16.

59 Beetham, *A Magazine of Her Own*, p.13.

60 Ibid, p.14.

61 Judith Butler, *Gender Trouble: Feminism and the Subversion of Identity* (London, Routledge, 1990), p.141.

62 Ibid., p.140.

63 'Shall I Go in for Nursing', *Home Chat*, LXXVI/981, p.5.

64 For example, see *Home Chat*, LXXVI/981 (3 January 1914), 'The Playbox', p.23; 'Gladys Owen's Tea Parties', p.35; *Home Chat*, LXXVI/983 (17 January 1914), 'The Playbox', p.119 and 'Gladys Owen, If You Came to Dinner on Thursday', p.131.

65 *Home Chat*, LXXVI/981, 982, 983.

66 *Home Chat*, LXXVII/1004 (13 June 1914), p.561.

67 See 'The Business of Marriage', *Home Chat*, LXXVI/982, p.49; *Home Chat*, LXXVI/981, p.45.

68 See, for example, Pugh, *Women and the Women's Movement in Britain*; Kingsley Kent, *Making Peace*; and Braybon and Summerfield, *Out of the Cage*.

69 *Home Chat*, LXXXII/1059 (3 July 1915), p.15.

70 *Home Chat*, LXXVIII/1017 (12 September 1914), p.490.

71 *Home Chat*, LXXVIII/1020 (3 October 1914).

72 For example, one described 'Life in the Army', and another showed Sir John French, Commander of the British army, on the cover: *Home Chat*, LXXVIII/1021 (10 October 1914), pp.41–2; *Home Chat*, LXXX/1036 (23 January 1915).

73 *Home Chat*, LXXX/1035, 1036, 1044 (16 January, 23 January, 20 March 1915), cover, pp.125, 441.

74 *Home Chat*, LXXX/1021 (10 October 1914), pp.45-51.

75 *Home Chat*, LXXXI/1048, p.119, *Home Chat*, LXXXII/1067, p.323.

76 *Home Chat*, LXXXI/1055, p.395.

77 *Home Chat*, LXXX/1042, cover image.

78   Mica Nava and Alan O'Shea, *Modern Times reflections on a century of English modernity* (London, Routledge, 1996), p.11.

79   See Braybon & Summerfield, *Out of the Cage*, p.75.

80   Marwick, *Women at War 1914–1918*, p.127.

81   See Walker, 'Vistas of pleasure' in Campbell Orr, *Women in the Victorian Art World*.

82   Beetham, *A Magazine of Her Own*, p.195.

83   *Home Chat*, LXXVIII/1017, pp.443–4.

84   *Home Chat*, LXXXI/1057, p.473.

85   *Home Chat*, LXXX/1044, p.455.

86   *Home Chat*, LXXVI/983, p.109.

87   *Home Chat*, LXXVI/982, p.65.

88   *Home Chat*, LXXVI/981, p.44.

89   *Home Chat*, LXXXII/1061 (17 July 1915), p.81.

90   *Home Chat* LXXXII/1061 (31 July 1915), p.171.

91   *Home Chat*, LXXXII/1061 (17 July 1915), p.81.

92   *Home Chat*, LXXXIV/1096 (18 March 1916), p.491.

93   *Home Chat*, LXXXIV/1096 (18 March 1916), p.491.

94   *Home Chat*, LXXXIV/1096, front cover.

95   Hereafter referred to as *The Queen* in the main text.

96   *The Queen, the Lady's Newspaper and Court Chronicle*, CXLIII/3723 (4 May 1918), pp.490–3.

97   *Vogue*, 15 September 1916, p.130.

98   See Sheila Rowbotham, *Hidden From History* (London, Pluto Press, 1973) for discussion of these themes.

99   Vron Ware, *Beyond the Pale: White Women, Racism and History* (London, Verso, 1992), p.37.

100   See Richard Dyer, *White* (London, Routledge, 1997), Ch. 3.

101   Ibid., p.113.

102   Ibid., p.87.

103   Suren Lalvani, 'Photography, Epistemology and the Body', quoted from Dyer, *White*, p.105.

104   See Charles L. Mowat, *Britain Between the Wars 1918–1940* (Cambridge, Methuen, 1987).

105   Dyer, *White*, p.86.

106   See 'Mars, Medals, and Matrons', *Vogue*, February 1917, and fashion feature *Vogue*, September 1916.

107   Ibid., p.33.

108   It is also worth noting that paper patterns in *Home Chat* cost a fraction of the price, at 3d.

4 Re-imagining the Feminine: Fashion, Modernity and Identity in Britain Between the Wars

During the 1920s and 1930s, the fashionable female body was the focus for a range of contradictory ideas about the nature of feminine identity. The broader context which framed this was women's shifting social and cultural roles, particularly their experience of modernity and their relative positions within inter-war patriarchy. Images of the sexually and socially emancipated lifestyles of specific groups of women were to be found in a number of popular cultural arenas. Fashion, in particular, was influential in representing some of the changes which had shaped and continued to shape women's lives. It was one of the 'welter of experiences and images that presented a world beyond the family, domestic service and the locality'.[1] It provided both working-class and middle-class women with a means to represent themselves as feminine, and in this respect fashion was a critical tool in defining identity as gender was renegotiated throughout the inter-war years.

A number of aspects of the fashion system contributed to this process of redefinition, including stylish advertising, illustration and photography in women's magazines, elegant fashion shops and department stores, and even the new clothing factories in which women increasingly gained employment. Most significant were the movies, in which silver-screen stars, especially from the USA, created highly glamorous female images. All of these were key sites where desirable and potentially transgressive feminine identities were formulated, engaged with and, to some extent, contested by women from different classes. One specific group of women, however, was at the forefront of change: 'in so far as there was a spirit of emancipation [it] affected the conduct of the young, and particularly young women'.[2] It was these women whose attitudes and values were to be scrutinised as their importance as consumers of clothes and popular forms of entertainment, such as dancing, music and cinema, began to be recognised.

Contemporary commentators and subsequent historians observed the significance of fashion as a sign of women's changing social, economic and political power. Writing in 1955, the historian Charles Loch Mowat made a direct link between social and economic factors and women's fashion in the 1920s when he suggested, 'After the war many women could not hope for marriage and many men could not afford it. This conjunction of circumstances affected manners – and women's fashions – so that femininity and the maternal instincts were kept firmly under heavy disguise.'[3] This particular analysis of fashion is one of a number. Sheila Rowbotham, in her influential feminist history, *Hidden From History* discussed the use of makeup in the 1920s, and drew a different conclusion to Mowat's, arguing instead that an exaggerated femininity became a guise: 'It was as if women were being forced to make their own mask to face the strange new masculine world they were invading'.[4] To Rowbotham and some feminist historians, 'the cultural attitudes of the twenties and thirties were remote from those of the Victorian era. It was not so much a reaction; it was rather that anti-feminism took on new social and cultural forms.'[5] In contrast, Sally Alexander sees the widespread engagement with the complexity of fashionable iconography by working-class as well as middle-class women, which perhaps distinguishes fashion in the 1920s and the 1930s from that of the preceding decade, as a mark of independence and as a characteristic of the search for a new sense of identity.[6] Her analysis points to the possibility of reading women's fashion in the 1920s and 1930s afresh, refusing the dominant interpretation articulated by feminists writing in the 1930s, such as Winifred Holtby, who in *Women and a Changing Civilisation* argued:

> The post-war fashion for short skirts, bare knees, straight, simple chemise-like dresses, shorts and pyjamas for sports and summer wear, cropped hair and serviceable shoes is waging a defensive war against this powerful movement to reclothe the female form in swathing trails and frills and flounces to emphasise the difference between men and women.[7]

In the context of the immense turmoil and insecurity generated by the First World War and by women's successful demand for the vote, femininity came under intense scrutiny between the wars. On the one hand, it signified a peaceful, alternative way forward following the ultimate masculine folly of war. On the other hand, discussions around femininity raised anxieties about women's roles as wives and mothers, and the price to be paid for their economic and personal independence, as well as foregrounding a host of issues about women's sexual identity and their relationships with men and with each other. At the same time, what it meant to be a woman and to be feminine were fiercely debated within feminist organisations, and by writers and commentators of both sexes. Fashion was an important arena for the creation not just of images of modernity but also for the articulation of gender, and to some extent class identities. This chapter will explore the inter-relationships between fashion, femininity and modernity in Britain between the wars. It will show the ways in which fashioning the female body involved women in the process of 're-imagining' themselves, and how they were also 'imagined' by others. Advertisers, retailers, film-makers and magazine editors, as well as fashion designers, identified the growing influence of female consumers, and part of this chapter will consider how these disparate, but related, interests attempted to 'locate' women as consumers of fashionable clothing.

Women's experiences of life in Britain between the wars were shaped by two major political events: the First World War and the success of the women's suffrage campaign. Negotiating the impact of these changes on their everyday lives presented women with a challenge. As Susan Kingsley Kent argued, 'public anxiety about women's place in society centred on work. Removing women from their wartime jobs to eliminate competition with men for work was regarded as one way to assure, as Ray Strachey put it, that everything could be as it had been before.'[8] In some respects, the inter-war years can be seen as a period of anti-feminism and political uncertainty, as the focus and momentum represented by the campaign for the vote was dissipated.[9] Rowbotham suggested that 'the sexual liberation of the early twenties was extremely superficial', and Deidre Beddoe argued that 'the reality is that socially and economically the lives of the vast majority of women remained much the same as before the First War. A woman's place was in the home and if she went out to work it was as a low paid worker.'[10] In contrast, more recent feminist historians Sally Alexander and Judy Giles have put forward a different interpretation. In discussing Margery Spring Rice's *Working-Class Wives* of 1939, Giles suggests that she, 'construct[s] the working-class woman as passive victim of forces beyond her control, fatalistic and stoical in her recognition that "life is hard"'.[11] Instead she proposes that 'the social and economic changes of the inter-war years provided the conditions in which it became possible for such women to construct alternate versions of their lives: versions that contest their representation as powerless victims and locate possibilities for change in their own agency'.[12]

Fashion provided women with an accessible cultural language to contest oppressive representations and to begin to construct new versions of their identities; inevitably these were shaped by the discourses of modernity. Women's cultural, as opposed to social and political lives were influenced as much by experiences within the home as by the exterior world of work, particularly their relationship to modernity, which was 'felt and lived in the most interior and private places'.[13] The social and cultural changes which characterised modernity between the wars offered both working-class and middle-class women new opportunities as producers and as consumers of an array of new products for the home and personal use. At the same time, modernity provided a cultural context in which it was possible for women to question dominant notions of 'femininity'. Modernity connected with femininity in particularly poignant ways. Stressing the conflict between two images which compete in the popular memory of the 1920s and 1930s – the unemployed male industrial worker and the fashionable young woman – Alexander links femininity to the future, to the glamorous modernity of the Hollywood screen idols, and masculinity to the past, to unemployment and the dying traditional industries of shipbuilding, mining and engineering: 'the cloth cap and spare frame of the unemployed man whose face and staring eyes still wrench pity from the onlooker; and the young girl – lipsticked, silk-stockinged, and dressed…"like an actress"'.[14]

Writers such as Sally Alexander and Alison Light have explored women's experience and engagement with modernity, and the relationship between notions of modernity and contemporary perceptions of the 'feminisation' of British social, economic and cultural life. Modernity marks out a space for both writers in which women renegotiated aspects of femininity, and in which feminine experiences came more sharply into focus. Indeed this increased 'feminisation' of cultural life was identified by several writers in the inter-war years, as women became increasingly visible in the labour market as workers in the new light industries and, most importantly, as consumers of domestic products: 'not only is the new working class in these new industries female, but the wants and needs which the new industries supply are feminine'.[15] However, for some writers both the impact of modernity and its apparent 'feminisation' were intensely problematic, and ultimately represented a form of cultural 'dumbing-down' which undermined class identities. Evident in George Orwell's novel *Coming Up for Air* and in his essay 'England Your England' is resentment against the identical rows of middle-class housing which 'fester all over the inner-outer suburbs'.[16] Orwell railed against modernity, particularly American-style, and the democratised or 'mass' society which inhabited the vast new wildernesses of glass and brick. He observed that 'in tastes, habits, manners and outlook the working class and the middle class are drawing together…It is a rather restless, culture-less life, centring round tinned food, *Picture Post*, the radio and the internal combustion engine.'[17] In *Coming Up for Air*, women, through the figure of Hilda, the main character's wife, represented and contributed to the erosion of class identities. From the impoverished middle class, Hilda's family never has money, but is always thinking about it. Family members have never done anything that can be termed 'real work', which for Orwell was shorthand for manual labour. Yet their aspirations for an indoor bathroom, their 'own' home, a radio and other 'modern' appliances signified social conformity and the encroachment of American methods of mass-production and consumption. In Orwell's writing, the impetus for consumption comes from women whose desires are small-minded and easily sated.

A number of other critics, writers and social observers shared Orwell's concerns. In *An English Journey*, J.B. Priestley famously contrasted the world of the arterial roads, suburbs, new factories and shiny cocktail bars in the South of England with industrial desolation and the demise of heavy manual labour in the North. Turning to Tyneside, he observed the 'scrag-ends of industrial life', but ignored the obvious symbols of modernity such as the new Tyne Bridge, opened in 1928, and the attempts at economic renewal already evident in several regions, including the Northeast.[18] Indeed the feminisation of cultural life was not just apparent in the South. Whereas Priestley had focused on a North/South divide, there was, as Alexander has argued, a clear gender division as young women in the disadvantaged regions, including Yorkshire, South Wales, Scotland and the Northeast, gained jobs in the new industries, as did young women in the Southeast. These jobs were to be found in new factories built along the large arterial roads which led out of large cities, such as the Great Western Road in London, and on new trading estates, such as that established in the Team Valley, Gateshead in 1938. These new industries often included clothing, and indeed in Middlesbrough, a Northeast town renowned for tailoring due to the skills of its large Jewish community, Henry Price built a new all-electric 'Rational Tailoring' factory to produce the 50-shilling men's suit on the strength of abundant cheap female labour. With decent jobs, young women in the North rivalled their southern counterparts as consumers of new fashions, makeup and entertainment.

Unaccompanied by men, these stylish young women were to be found out with their girlfriends across Britain, enjoying the local fairs, visiting the increasingly popular and available seaside resorts, and shopping for clothes on the expanding high street (Figure 4.1). Wearing fashionably short skirts and dresses (at or just above the knee), sheer silk stockings, cloche hats over cropped hair, these women were 'the visible shock troops of industrial re-structuring'.[19] Their prominence points to the increasing disparity, economically and in terms of lifestyles, between young single women in work and working-class men in the traditional industries whose jobs were being lost. These young women were at the height of modernity – single, independent, consumers – and they were dressed accordingly, in sharply defined 'modern' clothes which they wore with ease.

Such images of smart, well-dressed young women were highly evocative, and they reveal the way in which the lives of some groups of women changed drastically between the wars. Although the extent of women's emancipation and their engagement with modernity is questionable, particularly for older working-class and middle-class married women, it is evident that some

Figure 4.1: Women at the North East Coast Exhibition, Newcastle-upon-Tyne, 1929.
Reproduced by permission of Newcastle Libraries and Information Service.

women, especially those who were young and single and those who had some degree of economic independence, did experience more freedom than hitherto: 'girls growing up in the early years of this century experienced a widening of their social horizons which had not been available to their mothers'.[20] In the towns and cities, young women went out dancing unchaperoned, they bought and exchanged women's magazines, attended the cinema at least once a week, and avidly followed the latest fashionable styles: 'in this way, via the high street or the sewing machine, the mantle of glamour passed from the aristocrat and courtesan to the shop, office or factory girl via the film star'.[21] Sometimes with the advantage of the sewing machine, but often stitched by hand, working-class factory girls, such as the Pease Mill workers shown at the works dance in the mid-1920s, were able to produce fashionable clothes (Figure 4.2). Although not made from luxurious materials or elaborately decorated, the clothes worn by these young women were typical of the simple tubular dresses popular in the 1920s. This particular style, based on an essentially modernist line, was easy to copy, and could be adapted from existing clothes. With bobbed and shingled haircuts, but without the paraphernalia worn by their mother's generation for such social occasions, these young women factory workers drew on the language of modern fashion to represent their engagement with the contemporary world.

In a number of ways, these women challenged dominant notions of femininity and rendered impossible any return to pre-war ideals. Their lack of compliance with traditional values and standards, and the perception that they cared only for 'having a good time' provoked concern from across the political spectrum. Indeed it has been argued that the denial of the vote until

Figure 4.2: Women workers at Pease's Mill, Darlington, mid-1920s.
Reproduced by permission of Darlington Borough Council.

1928 to the youthful flapper revealed not only 'a fear of how women would use the vote if they were the majority of the electorate but also a deep-seated concern about the younger, sexually active woman'.[22] An advertisement in the women's magazine *Britannia and Eve* from 1929 epitomised this (Figure 4.3). Advertising cigarettes, and accompanied by a rhyme, 'Our New Electorate... Vote For Abdullah', this depicted a young women with bobbed hair and short cocktail dress slouching and casually smoking a cigarette. Titled 'Miss Infatuation', this 'liberated' young woman represented an important new market for cigarettes.

> It would kill poor Papa if the country went red,
> Yet I mean to vote Communist, Imogen said;
> My home and allowance are nothing to me
> Since I sat next Bert Hunks at a Bolsheviks Tea!
>
> His face is unshaven, but earnest and thin,
> If he seizes the Banks a New World will begin;
> Though Papa may be penniless – think what a joke
> When Abdulla's Delight is a Communal Smoke.[23]

Provocatively, the rhyme and the image depicted a young woman, infatuated by both 'Bert Hunks' and cigarettes, with little sense of value for the hard-won vote, and foolish enough to dally in radical politics. This was over 10 years after women over thirty had gained the vote, and shortly after the franchise had been extended to all women. The assumed superficiality of this type of young woman attracted censure from critics of the right and the left. However, as this advertisement made clear, fashion was a crucial visual device for evoking this challenge. In the process of cutting their hair, putting

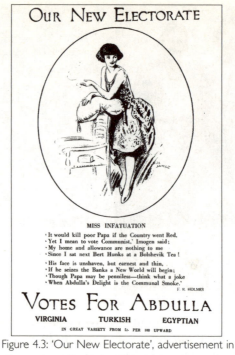

Figure 4.3: 'Our New Electorate', advertisement in
Britannia and Eve, June 1929. Authors' copyright.

on makeup, wearing the striking new fashions and smoking in public, 'dress
or self-presentation [became] ... a symbol of defiance, a gesture of independence ... a statement of individuality, of distance from siblings and parents'.[24]

Interpreting fashion gave women the opportunity to engage with the
modern world and to question feminine identities in a public as well as a
private way. Uniquely, it combined the interior domestic world of the home,
the private world of dressing the body, and the exterior worlds of shopping
and working. It afforded women the means to signify their involvement with
modern social life – with the city and town, with some measure of personal
choice and independence, and with the contemporary pleasures of shops,
magazines, the cinema and dancing. It provided a powerful symbol of
modernity in a number of specific ways: the emphasis on day and leisure-
wear pointed to freer, less formal lifestyles; style, cut and fashionable
iconography were a testament to the influence of Hollywood glamour and
particular screen idols such as Clara Bow, Greta Garbo, Joan Crawford and
Jean Harlow; and new methods of manufacture, synthetic materials, stylish
advertising and lower prices were indicators of the impact of the modern
production strategies of Taylorism and the effectiveness of American
marketing and retailing techniques.[25] Dressed in smart, well-cut clothes Lily
Robinson, Jean Dawson and Elsie Hogg, photographed while out walking,

Figure 4.4: Lily Robinson, Jean Dawson and Elsie Hogg (left to right), out walking in Tynemouth, mid-1930s. Reproduced by permission of Pat Maher.

represent this (Figure 4.4). All three young women wore highly fashionable clothes which demonstrated their knowledge of the latest looks, and Hogg, in particular, with stylish clutch bag and shoes, carefully groomed hair and makeup, tailored suit and striped sweater, combined the minimalist sophistication of Coco Chanel with the glamour of Katherine Hepburn. As an aspect of material culture, then, fashion was as potent an image of modernity as a new suburban house or an electric iron. It had added importance and significance in that it served the dual purpose of allowing women to signal their questioning of sexual identity and femininity at the same time as highlighting the ambiguities of women's social, political and economic positions.

Sexual identities and gender differences were critically debated in the aftermath of the First World War, which had been 'nothing if not a transgression of categories'.[26] In such a context, the impetus was to set things straight: to re-establish appropriate relationships, including those between the sexes. Feminists who resisted such moves, or those who tried to keep feminist concerns on the agenda, were criticised: 'Prewar egalitarian feminism, with its suggestion of sex war, seems to have been associated in the public mind with a renewal of the massive conflict so recently ended'.[27] Increasingly it seemed that women had to negotiate their way carefully so as not to be seen to compete with men or to provoke their anger. As Winifred Holtby wrote, 'A sense of bitterness infects many public utterances, speeches and articles, made on the subject of women's position in the state'.[28] Feminism responded to such concerns by splintering and fragmenting. The pre-war generation of feminists, which included Holtby, remained committed to 'equal rights' feminism, in contrast to younger feminists such as Eleanor Rathbone, President of NUSEC (National Union of Societies of Equal Citizenship), and Mary Stocks, who embraced what was called 'new' feminism, which tried to appeal to a broader spectrum of women: those in trade unions and those in the home.[29] Implicit in the writings and convictions of the new feminists was the notion that women had now achieved equality with men, and that there 'is a permanent difference between the average woman and the average man, due to their natural qualities and vocations'.[30] A crucial issue for feminists and social commentators between the wars was sexuality, and much of the debate was couched in Freudian terms. Following the translation of Freud's essays into English and their publication in Britain in 1922, aspects of Freudian psychoanalytic theory became increasingly popularised, particularly in the context of defining sex roles. It was utilised by a number of sexologists to theorise sexual relationships between men and women which were presented as a battle in which 'woman is the enemy of man, whom she constantly combats by every means at her disposal'.[31] Freudian theories were marshalled to legitimise the re-establishment of conservative notions of appropriate relations between the sexes and to reinforce specific ideals of sexual fulfilment within marriage.[32]

Influenced by Freud and his followers, sexuality was a concern to the younger generation of feminists, although Sheila Rowbotham has argued that 'sexual emancipation in the twenties and thirties remained confined to a narrow privileged section of society'.[33] However, a book such as Marie Stopes's *Married Love*, published in 1918 and which discussed sexual fulfilment alongside birth control, was highly influential – it had sold 400,000 copies by 1923.[34] It put forward the idea that women could gain sexual pleasure within marriage, and that marriage should be a partnership in which both men and women gained satisfaction. Significantly, Stopes's work repudiated the notion of women's sexual passivity, and even middle-class women's magazines such as *Good Housekeeping* were keen to persuade women that they had 'sex desires and that these desires were not wicked; that to repress them was as difficult and dangerous to women as to men, and that they need no longer pretend that all they wanted was at most mother-hood, when it was quite as natural for them to want loverhood'.[35]

During the 1920s, ideas which questioned sexual identity were especially appealing to the young, who were in revolt against the ideals of the pre-war generation, whom they held responsible for the hypocrisy and carnage of the First World War. Within such a context, lesbianism was more openly discussed, especially following the scandal which surrounded Radclyffe Hall's book *The Well of Loneliness* (published in 1928 but promptly banned as obscene).[36] Although this novel has been criticised as sentimental and for representing a fundamentally flawed analysis of lesbian identity, it was an important attempt to account for sexual feelings which were not heterosexual. Hall accepted Havelock Ellis's view of lesbianism as sexual inversion, but nevertheless gave an account of how women might live together in relationships which were intimate and sexual. Such a proposition was clearly transgressive of and challenging to patriarchy. However, by the 1930s the emphasis on sexual fulfilment – either heterosexual or homosexual – had been re-packaged along more conventional lines for married women, and although there remained a number of radicals, such as Stella Browne and Dora Russell, who represented a socialist-feminist position by demanding women's complete sexual freedom and the right to choose with regard to abortion, they were undoubtedly in the minority.

For many women, any debate about sex focused on the highly practical matter of birth control, which became more respectable, especially for the middle classes, through the publication of Stopes's *Married Love*.[37] Contraception was more widely discussed in popular magazines, and was available to some women with the opening of her clinics, the first in London in 1921.[38] However, in *Working Class Wives*, Margery Spring Rice indicted the state for not making contraceptives available to the 1250 women studied for her report.[39] As she noted, the fear of unwanted pregnancies was the biggest obstacle to any plan for women's sexual pleasure in marriage. Although no new methods of contraception appeared in Britain between the wars, the adoption of contraceptive devices became more widespread among the working class as older women were concerned that their daughters should not face the same health problems from continual pregnancies that they had suffered:[40] 'By the end of the 1930s more and more young women were able to refuse their mothers' lives, not because they had new jobs, and cheap clothes, but because they could have fewer children'.[41] The shift to smaller families (2.2 live births by the late 1920s, as opposed to 5–6 in the mid-nineteenth century) preceded innovations in birth control, and was instead dependent on changing attitudes and aspirations:

> The life experiences of many of the young women of the 1920s and 1930s underlines the point. Many had been lifted out of the routine of home life during the war; contacts with large numbers of other girls probably speeded up the flow of information about birth control; easier social relations doubtless concentrated minds on the avoidance of pregnancy; and higher income raised expectations for the future.[42]

In contrast, Elizabeth Roberts found in her study of working-class women from Preston, Lancaster and Barrow that although women claimed to have close relationships with their mothers, as young women growing up they were remarkably ignorant of sex.[43] Pearl Jephcott's survey *Girls Growing Up*, of 1942, suggested that information about sex barely impacted on the young working girl, although occasionally a book on birth control might do the rounds of boys and girls.[44] Instead, she discussed the way in which ideas about sex were framed by the cinema. According to Jephcott, the language and phrases which girls used to describe sex came from Hollywood films: 'A girl of this age [fourteen years] who has just seen and very much enjoyed the picture *Blossoms in the Dust*, is perfectly at home with a word like "illegitimacy". She talks quite naturally of a star whose "kisses are supposed to thrill you through and through".'[45]

Hollywood was a significant influence on young women, as were women's magazines, both of which were within the reach of working-class girls, although both types of media had their critics. In *Women and a Changing Civilisation*, Winifred Holtby recognised the appeal of the cinema: 'When lives are restricted, the routine of work and leisure unvaried, limited and dull, it is not surprising that the vivid emotional romance of the Screen ... should capture the imagination', but she regretted the lack of interest in politics, religion and social services shown by young women.[46] The cinema was perceived as part of that same process of standardisation and Americanisation of culture that Orwell's and Priestley's writings identified. Such views were reinforced by the writings of the Frankfurt group of theorists, particularly Max Horkheimer and Theodor Adorno, whose essays in the inter-war years and subsequently attacked the new 'culture industries', which included the cinema and other aspects of popular culture such as music and dancing.[47] For these theorists, such popular culture was standardised, homogeneous and conformist, and located the participant as a passive consumer whose energies were dissipated by its triviality. Significantly, fashion was one of these forms of mass culture, and it is telling that Holtby criticises 'twopenny fashion journals and inexpensive stores, [in which] it is possible for one fashion to affect a whole hemisphere with no distinction of class and little of pocket'.[48] Discussing the Frankfurt theorists, Mica Nava suggests that their position represents 'a virulent denigration of ordinary audiences', and in a powerful critique, she argues:[49]

> Ironically one way of reading these views is to see them as evidence of men's passivity as they witness the reorientation of women's desires away from the home to the seductive environment of the cinema and stores ... Mass culture emerges then as the despised yet alluring rival of the displaced man. The insistence of the cultural critics on the passivity of the consumer can be reread as denial, as a disavowal of the profound anxiety about loss and displacement that mass culture seems to engender.[50]

Such a reading of the left's attack on mass culture needs to be understood in the context of the recent work of Alison Light and others who have argued that popular culture in Britain between the wars was in some ways 'feminine'. The cinema and fashion were aspects of this 'feminised' mass culture, and women's consumption of these remained problematic for the left and for feminists throughout the period.

For some feminists, such as Holtby and Margaret Haig (Lady Rhondda), these forms of mass culture were part of a backlash against women which they believed was evident not only in fashion and film, but also in the work of writers such as G.B. Shaw, D.H. Lawrence and H.G. Wells. More alarmingly, they noted the assimilation of these views in the writings of women: 'Read 80% of the moderately good novels by women today, and you will find in them the echo of the beliefs of D.H. Lawrence ... Women, they seem to be telling us all the time, must rest every hope they have on personal relations.'[51]

To the pre-war generation of feminists including Rebecca West, Cicely Hamilton, Vera Brittain and Winifred Holtby, it appeared that the public display of fashionable clothes, cosmetics, dancing and the cinema, the pursuit of marriage, and the intense interest in heterosexual sex marked a return to forms of femininity which they had fought against in their political and private lives. As the 1930s progressed, they were to be increasingly worried by the Fascist vision for womanhood, articulated by Oswald Moseley 'as different but equal'. Within this context, the older generation of middle-class feminists saw the fashion changes of the 1920s and 1930s as one of a number of reactionary forces which aimed to differentiate clearly men from women along conventional gender lines. However, for many young working-class women, feminism was hardly the issue. Instead, making choices about how to spend their money and choosing which glamorous styles they should buy or make was symbolic of their hard-won economic independence.

In *Girls Growing Up*, Pearl Jephcott's account of the lives of young working girls from a number of British cities and towns in the 1930s, it is clear that the single most important factor was work; as she put it, 'all kinds of new possibilities are opened to the girl as soon as she has a job'.[52] Describing the lives of two fifteen-year-olds – one a Birmingham factory worker and the other a 'North Country nursemaid' – Jephcott describes how the first was paid £1 17 shillings 3d plus 4 shillings 9d overtime (£2 2 shillings in total), the second 8 shillings per week. All their wages were handed over to their mothers, but they were given money back as pocket money (14 shillings 9d and 4 shillings 6d respectively), some of which they spent on dancing (1 shilling 6d), the cinema (10d), cigarettes (6d), ice creams (4d), cakes (6d) and bus rides (10d). Their mothers paid for their clothes, but they were allowed to choose them, and one bought a bathing suit with her own money.[53] Disdain for modernity and mass culture is evident in Jephcott's writing as she comments, 'both girls are then very much at the mercy of the commercial world which in the main puts before them second-rate goods, cinemas rather than theatres, trash magazines rather than books, and synthetic foods and materials rather than the genuine article'.[54]

Irrespective of left-wing and feminist disapproval of mass culture, Hollywood glamour was the most potent visual media accessible to young working-class women. For 10d or less each week they could go to the movies or buy cinema magazines such as *Picturegoer*.[55] For women, going to the cinema was one of the main delights of life, and it ranked on a par with dancing and window-shopping as sites of female pleasure. It was appealing as a cheap form of entertainment, and it was unconstrained by class-specific notions of British good taste. In fact it was the antithesis of this: flashy and brash, drawing inspiration from glamorised American lifestyles and aspirations, and visually dependent on a popularised and bastardised form of modernism derived from Art Deco and Moderne styles.

Hollywood glamour represented a form of high femininity which not only exaggerated but parodied the desirable upper-middle-class femininity associated with British film stars.[56] As a look, it was widely disseminated: for example, appearing at Darlington's Phoenix Little Theatre in 1934, the actress Nita drew on these visual codes to present a highly glamorous image

Figure 4.5: The actress Nita, starring at the Phoenix
Little Theatre in 1936. Reproduced by permission
of Darlington Borough Council.

(Figure 4.5). Sharply drawn eyebrows and lashes, perfectly painted dark lips and waved bobbed hair were combined with a cossack-style velvet jacket edged with fur to evoke the mystery and 'otherness' of Hollywood star Greta Garbo. Even her name, Nita, contributed to this. Nita's brand of femininity was artificial and larger-than-life, far removed from the realities of life in a Northern town. For young working-class women, such glamorous images, makeup and smoking were important symbols of rebellion against family expectations and middle-class aspirations; as Judy Giles put it, 'the cheekiness so deplored by middle-class observers acted as a means of asserting a self-image that refused to be defined by either reference to ideals of feminine sexuality or by reference to the conventions of "ladylike" behaviour'.[57] Arguably, identification with Hollywood glamour marked a refusal to slip seamlessly into one's allotted place as wife and mother, and not surprisingly it was most strongly associated with young working girls, those who before marriage had some freedom to indulge their fantasies:

> the intelligent girl of fifteen who spends from 8 a.m. to 5 p.m. in hammering three nails into a cardboard box cannot be satisfied by such a life. She searches for vicarious satisfaction and she finds it in the diamond stealing, blackmail and breath-taking adventures of the gangster film … and in the good times, lovely clothes, and 'kisses that thrill' which poured out of Hollywood.[58]

It was mainly during adolescence, that brief period between childhood and adulthood, 'when everything seems possible and identity is in flux, when the imagination yields to convention and restraint only with difficulty' that film and fashion provided women with an opportunity to transgress the norms of femininity.[59] Jephcott described a typical fifteen-year-old girl working in a London office who had visited the cinema several times a week for the last five years, and bought *Picturegoer* on a regular basis. Another young girl who formed part of Jephcott's study 'spends her energies, her precious free time, her hard-earned money and her youthful enthusiasms on stars of the Carmen Miranda brand'.[60] However, as Jephcott observed, long hours and boredom still curtailed the youthful freedoms of machinists in Glasgow, Manchester and Birmingham, as did the responsibility placed on girls to help with siblings and housework at home.

Young working girls sometimes watched the same film two or three times a week in order to get the look right for a particular star, which would then be carefully constructed at home: 'The high heels and tilt of the hat gave the illusion for a moment of wealth, of abundance, of being like Greta Garbo or Ginger Rodgers'.[61] As Jane Gaines and Charlotte Herzog have shown, Hollywood studios were increasingly adept at promoting particular star looks and marketing related products by linking up with designated stores.[62] However, women were also able to copy styles from film magazines, and they could buy paper patterns from companies such as Butterick which offered copies of stars' outfits.[63] Women were also highly discerning in their identification with particular stars and constructions of feminine beauty. The dyed hair, wide mannish jackets, figure-hugging gowns and smoking of stars such as Joan Crawford, Bette Davis, Greta Garbo and Jean Harlow were skilfully copied and adapted to convey feminine images which jarred with the accepted norms of 'British' femininity which seemed dull and old-fashioned. Marlene Dietrich's blatant sexuality, Katherine Hepburn's masculinised dress and Carmen Miranda's naked midriff and swirling skirts were transgressive of conventional feminine norms, and they inevitably contributed to the view that femininity was not fixed, but precarious, negotiable and malleable.

Although such sexual transgression was not explicit, there was discussion of characters and plots in movie magazines which hinted at such meanings, and some cinematic representations were fairly blatant. Greta Garbo in *Queen Christina* (R. Mamoulian, 1933), Marlene Dietrich in *Blonde Venus* (J. von Sternberg, 1932), and Katherine Hepburn in *Christopher Strong* (D. Arzner, 1933) played roles which highlighted ambiguities around sexual identity through oblique references to lesbianism or by taking on masculine-type roles. In *Christopher Strong*, Hepburn plays Cynthia Darrington, a world-champion aviator who, according to Annette Kuhn, 'transgresses male discourse through the element of sex-role reversal inherent in her characterisation'.[64] In other films, such as *Front Page Woman* (M. Curtis, 1935) with Bette Davis, *The Wild Party* (D. Arzner, 1929) with Clara Bow, and *Mr Deeds Goes to Town* (F. Capra, 1936) with Jean Arthur, women challenged dominant sexual stereotypes even if they ultimately came to conform. Although Hollywood's questioning of femininity and sexual identity was usually compromised by the needs of the marketplace, these films nevertheless provided powerful representations of women challenging assumptions about their lives, attributes, roles and desires in an unprecedented way. Revealing attitudes which were typical of many social commentators of the left, Jephcott, who recommended Soviet-style regulations to counter what she saw as the poor example set by Hollywood films, argued that the tastes formed by film companies 'exalt violence, vulgarity, sentimentality, and false psychology. Veronica Lake and Lana Turner do more for the girl than merely set her hair style'.[65]

In his study of cinema and society in Britain between 1930 and 1939, Jeffrey Richards argues 'that while a large proportion of the population at large went to the cinema occasionally, the enthusiasts were young, working-class, urban and more often than not female'.[66] Citing a number of sources, Richards argued that generally married women went more often than their husbands, and that of the adult audience for the cinema 75 per cent was female.[67] The cinema was designed to appeal to women in a number of ways, not just in relation to their aspirations to dress and look like the stars. The physical experience of the cinema space was a revelation to women used to few luxuries at home: 'The glamorous interiors of British cinemas … provided the cultural space for the consumption of Hollywood's glamorous femininity'.[68] Cinema design in the 1920s and 1930s was often spectacular, and frequently opulent, glistening with chrome, glass and highly polished veneered woods. Heavily decorated with modernistic, jazz-age motifs and exotic styles drawn from 'other' cultures such as Ancient Egypt or North Africa, it also combined new technologies to stimulate the senses of sight, sound and touch. Women were particularly susceptible to the pleasures of cinema-going 'responsible for the domestic space at home, and thus acutely aware of its limitations, women could thus be relied upon to respond to the promise of luxury offered by cinemas'.[69] In this respect, the sheer visual display of cinemas provided women with a form of pleasure which was gendered, in that the lavish interior designs appealed to their roles as arbiters of taste and consumers of furnishings within the home. Since the nineteenth century, women's roles, particularly in the middle class, were clearly linked to arranging and decorating the home as a safe haven to shield their families from the corruption of the outside world.[70] By the inter-war years, as the production and consumption of goods for the home increased, women from the skilled working class and lower-middle class were targeted by magazines such as *Good Housekeeping* (established 1922) as potential new consumers of home furnishings and ornamental goods. This form of consumption was domestic, and linked to one of women's primary roles within patriarchal ideology as 'angel in the home'. However, the cinema provided one of the few public spaces in which women could experience the pleasures of a type of consumption which was predicated on gratuitous luxury and sensory escapism, but at the same time connected to their gendered roles as homemakers.

The physicality of the cinema, the visual style of the films, and the star images, although on the one hand reaffirming stereotypical aspects of femininity, provided a context in which women could 'imagine' themselves as female in ways which ultimately challenged the patriarchy. Young women appropriated these symbols of femininity, but sometimes used them in provocative and subversive ways. Hollywood glamour provided the visual language with which to do this, and Hollywood film provided the role models, albeit problematic ones. In the process of dressing up and creating a fashionable image, young women stepped briefly outside their normal lives, as their film heroines had done:

> The cheap trappings of glamour were seized on by many young women in the 1920s and 1930s, frustrated in their wish for further education, yearning to escape the domestic treadmill of their mothers' lives, haunted by the fantasy, not of the prostitute as in the nineteenth century, but by the glamorous screen heroine who paradoxically could be you, the girl next door.[71]

The pleasures experienced by women in the luxurious new cinemas had few other counterparts in the public realm.[72] The new department stores were early examples,[73] but in the inter-war years, new purpose-built dance halls were opened, with names like Carlton, Mecca, Locarno and Palais de Dance, which were similar in visual style to the cinemas.[74] The dance halls were relatively cheap, and young women would go once or twice a week. Importantly, 'When the girl goes dancing it means that she can wear a smart frock and good stockings and try to look glamorous before her equals'.[75] Like the cinemas, dance halls and the music associated with the new craze for dancing attracted criticism. To the conservative-minded, it was blatantly physical (by implication sexual), and tainted by its association with working-class British culture and with the music emanating from African American communities in cities in the North of the USA and from the American South.[76] To those on the left, it was yet another example of the dissipation of working-class cultures:

> The dance hall offers the company of young people, an opportunity for rhythmical movement, and again, makes little demand on the dancer's mental capacity. There is nothing that is creative here, nothing that puts responsibility on young people or makes demands of them as members of society.[77]

Such comments reveal a serious misunderstanding of the importance of dancing and music to young men and women between the wars. As an article in *Picture Post* from 4 March 1939 shows, dancing captured the imagination of those who had few other opportunities for creative activity. This article described a day in the life of a 'Nippy' (as the waitresses at the Lyons' teashops were known). 'Young, attractive, hard-working, enthusiastic', there were 7600 Nippies by 1939, who had come from across the country to work mainly in the Southeast.[78] For long hours, starting at 8.30am and finishing at 5.30pm, she earned on average 32 shillings (25 shillings wage and 7 shillings tips). From this she allocated 8 shillings 6d for a room; 3 shillings 7d for bus fares; 1d a day for the laundry; 1d per week for the white cap, and 1 shilling 3d for health insurance and unemployment contribution. With two meals provided daily by Lyons, her weekly expenditure of just over 14 shillings, left her with 18 shillings, some of which would have been sent back to her family. Accompanying a series of photographs, the *Picture Post* narrative unfolds to describe how:

> Back Home: She rests before going out...She has a little sleep before she begins her day as a pretty young woman...She gets ready to enjoy herself...she is going to a dance...But first she spends a half-hour with the hairdresser...She meets her friends...No longer a Nippy, but a well-dressed and self-possessed young woman, enjoying an evening out.[79]

Getting ready for 'the dance' and going out, this young woman found the opportunity to be independent (Figure 4.6). Away from the pressures of work

Figure 4.6: A Lyons' Teashop 'Nippy' at a dance,
Picture Post, 4 March 1939.

and the watchful gaze of the family, this brief interlude in her day opened up a space in which, potentially, she could re-invent herself. Economic independence was the essential prerequisite for this, although fashion offered an accessible and exciting way of rendering this visual. With a new permed hairstyle and wearing a satin, bias-cut evening gown, this 'well-dressed and self-possessed young woman' drew on the language of Hollywood glamour, which in the 1930s was simultaneously conformist and transgressive, through the images of stars such as Katherine Hepburn, Jean Arthur, Greta Garbo and Jean Harlow.

Women's engagement with fashion was facilitated in a number of ways between the wars: there were opportunities for them to work in the new fashion retail outlets and in the recently built clothing factories, as well as to buy and make their own clothes. During the 1920s and 1930s, fashion retailing in Britain was transformed by the expansion of department stores and variety chain or multiple stores such as Marks & Spencer.[80] Design features for these new stores and for new department stores were drawn directly from the USA and they aimed to appeal directly to the female consumer as well as to make shopping modern and more rational in the organisation and design of stores. Large expanses of glass, for more spectacular window displays, island counters to show the goods better, and brighter lighting were essential features of the new shops. Hairdressers, tea lounges, rest rooms and dance bands were all planned to appeal to the female consumer. Like cinemas, the large department stores were regularly remodelled with marble lining, exotic wood veneering, and gilt detailing to create stylish departments for women's clothes.[81] In department stores such as Selfridges on London's Oxford Street and Fenwick on Northumberland St, Newcastle-upon-Tyne, clothing ranged from *couture* originals and top-quality copies catering for the upper classes to much more modest garments which showed the influence of the latest styles from Paris and Hollywood and were accessible to a middle-class if not a working-class market.[82]

Given the huge expansion in the range of shops from which women could make their clothing purchases, it was still the case that social class remained the critical factor in determining where they actually shopped and what they bought. Although stores such as Marks & Spencer brought better-quality clothing within the grasp of working-class and middle-class women, for the former, purchasing from such stores still represented a special investment, one not made regularly. For many working-class women, home dressmaking was the main way in which to acquire new clothes. It was supplemented to some extent by mail-order-catalogue purchasing from companies such as Littlewoods and Great Universal Stores, which had solid markets, particularly in the North, for their particular brand of selling through agents and mail order delivery. But for young women, a machine-made garment complete with a manufacturer's or retailer's label was highly prized as a symbol of fashionability and modernity.

Many families possessed or had access to a sewing machine, and with the aid of paper patterns available with most women's magazines, or equipped with a good eye for sketching from shop windows, women became adept at designing, cutting and making their own clothes.[83] This particular skill, which was supplemented by knitting, was often taught to working-class girls in domestic service.[84] For women with a little more money to spend, it was possible to take a fashion photograph or illustration and a length of fabric to a local dressmaker, who could make up the garment to a high standard. Department stores across Britain had extensive sections dedicated to the needs of the home dressmaker; these included Marshall and Snelgrove, John Lewis, Dickins and Jones and Whiteleys in London, Kendal Milne in Manchester, Fenwick and Bainbridge in Newcastle, and Binns in Darlington, Sunderland and Middlesbrough selling fabric and all haberdashery goods.

Fenwick had an annual 'sewing week' in the 1920s and 1930s, during which it encouraged home dressmakers. Many women, particularly those who had had some formal training before marriage, would continue to make clothes from home after marriage, to supplement the family income.[85] Providing another layer of dressmaking services were independent drapers, dressmakers and milliners, who could be found in many small towns and villages.[86] Significantly, these were increasingly under threat, as national multiple stores such as Marks & Spencer, British Home Stores, Littlewoods and C&A spread in the 1930s.[87] These multiples were important in other ways, in that they brought modernity to the high streets of towns and cities across Britain. Marks & Spencer, for example, introduced a number of distinctly modern features, including highly streamlined shop-fronts in green and gold, new selling techniques and the merchandising of standardised products, and shop window displays and promotions which were more unified, thus reinforcing a very specific fashionable look. All of these contributed to a widening of access to fashion, and at the same time facilitated women's engagement with different aspects of modernity.

Clearly, women's relationship to fashion, and by implication modernity and femininity, in the inter-war period was complex. The consumption of stylish clothes was encouraged by the cinema, by new dance crazes and by the new shops and ways of shopping, as well as by the greater accessibility of fashion information. However, women's knowledge of fashion came not just from wearing and making fashionable clothes, but by working with fashion. Work was a crucial site in which desirable feminine identities were contested in Britain between the wars. Due to essentialist notions of their skills in the workplace, women found jobs readily available in the new factories which produced cheaper, mass-produced clothing, as well as in the expanding fashion retailing sector. Although historically large numbers of women had been employed in the retail and clothing trades, gender still marked out clear differences for pay and employment prospects. Women's employment in fashion retailing and clothing production was shaped by a continuation and extension of practices established before 1914, in particular the sexual division of labour. Women took on jobs which were designated unskilled, whilst those jobs deemed skilled, such as pattern-making and cutting remained in male hands. As in other industries, the First World War had had a critical affect on women's employment in these industries which, combined with changes in the 1920s and 1930s, served to transform their work.[88] During the First World War, women sales assistants, dressmakers and tailoresses had taken on work previously done by men, and with trade-union support their wage levels had improved. The main unions to which women belonged were the National Amalgamated Union of Shop Assistants (NAUSA), which as well as sales assistants, catered for dressmakers and milliners employed by retailers; the Amalgamated Society of Cooperative Employees and Commercial Workers (ASCECW), whose members were mainly co-operative employees; the United Garment Workers (UGW); and the Amalgamated Society of Tailors and Tailoresses (ASTT). The UGW was made up of any workers, 'male or female, who are engaged in any of the occupations incidental to the manufacture of male and female clothing or attire', whereas the ASTT only admitted to its membership craftsmen or journeymen tailors.[89] Female membership of these unions in 1919 was substantial: on the production side, the UGW had 100,000 members, of which 75,000 were women, the ASTT had 20,000, of which half were women, whereas on the retailing side the NAUSA had 80,600, of which 35,300 were women, and the AUCECW had 87,000, of which 33,700 were women.[90]

It was primarily de-skilling which allowed larger numbers of women into the new factories equipped with new technologies for making cheaper, standardised clothes. As Wilson has argued, 'A further swing to factory production further broke down the divisions between the skilled tailor, the semi-skilled workers in tailoring shops, and the factory workers and sweated outworkers'.[91] In the 1930s, menswear, for example, was both mass-produced and made-to-measure by firms such as Montague Burton of London, the County Tailoring Company of Leeds and Prices Tailors of Middlesbrough.[92] Dubbed 'rational tailoring', Henry Price's 'Fifty Shilling Tailor' was the archetypal modernist clothing manufacturer, promising a fixed price and a fixed standard of values in tailoring. Opened in 1937, the Middlesbrough factory employed only female machinists (Figure 4.7). In this all-electric factory, row upon row of women undertook 'light' industrial work which undercut the work of local traditional male tailors. Along with the large number of women working in the office, Henry Price's new labour force epitomised the gendering of modernity in the 1920s and 1930s. The rationalism of the factory organisation, the use of new technologies for power tools and garment construction, the widespread deployment of women machinists and office workers to undertake 'light' work all contributed to the de-skilling of formerly skilled male tailoring jobs. Although there was substantial talk of women taking men's jobs in this period, a characteristic of working-class women's work was that it was comparatively low-paid and sexually segregated. Working-class women took jobs in new industries in which men would not work: those requiring skills and qualities perceived to be female, such as dexterity and the ability to withstand repetitive boring work. The experiences and roles of these women brought a specifically 'feminine' dimension to the modernity of these new industries, which served to undermine the masculine identity associated with work in the heavy, traditional industries. Jephcott described girls of between fourteen and sixteen working in these new highly mechanised factories producing one component in a complex system of

Figure 4.7: Women machinists at Henry Price's Fifty Shilling Tailors Ltd, Middlesbrough, 1937.
Reproduced by permission of the Dorman Museum, Middlesbrough Borough Council.

mass-production: 'She puts the power on with her foot, so that her hands are free to stitch together two pieces of narrow tape…A girl of fourteen will do this work from eight in the morning until twelve o'clock and again from one o'clock until five, day after day, and week after week.'[93] Such work was undoubtedly dull and repetitive but, crucially, gave girls as young as fourteen a sense of identity as 'earners', and in this respect gave them a different outlook to that of their mothers and grandmothers.

Women employees also formed an equally significant sector of the fashion retailing industry. As Susan Porter Benson has argued: 'Managers selected saleswomen both for their cheapness in the labour force and for their "female" personality characteristics which coincided with the skills of selling: empathy, habits of persuasion instead of command, and a homely familiarity with the merchandise'.[94]

They worked in department stores, multiple stores, and in smaller drapers, dressmakers and milliners. In these roles they were highly visible to the public as workers and earners. It was not uncommon to find women heading departments, although as stores amalgamated and increased in size during the 1930s men replaced women as departmental heads, except in those sections thought to require particular female skills, such as buying and welfare.[95] Nevertheless, ladies' clothing sections in large department stores were often staffed almost entirely by women.

Domestic service was still a common occupation for women, but it had become increasingly unpopular since the First World War as other types of work became available.[96] The choice of work for working-class women expanded with the development of the newer industries. The situation for middle-class women could be quite different. Often these women were better educated, attending secretarial and teaching colleges or training in offices, shops and hospitals, and consequently work could be better paid and more satisfying.[97] Generally, then, both working-class and middle-class women took on better-paid work in fashion industries. They had more job opportunities as semi-skilled machinists, typists and secretaries in factory and store offices, and in retailing. However, although work was an integral part of the lives of young working-class women, after marriage – still their main goal – it was relinquished. As Beddoe has argued, 'the typical woman worker was not only young, but she was single'.[98] On the whole, women workers tended to be single for one of three reasons; they gave up work upon marriage (sometimes voluntarily, but often compulsorily), they remained single, or they were widowed. In 1931, 40 per cent of women in the age group 15–59 were single.

Working-class women were expected to work before marriage to contribute to the family income, and they 'tipped up' their wages each week to their parents. Nevertheless, most young women had some disposable income, which they used for going out to the cinema and dancing, and buying magazines and dress fabrics. For some younger single women, expectations were changing. Work, some measure of financial responsibility, and more involvement in the world outside the home were tangible indicators of women's new roles. In this respect, the feminisation of British cultural, economic and social life was not merely about the interior world of home, family and domestic consumption, as perceived by writers such as George Orwell, it was also about women's engagement with modernity as workers and individual consumers of clothes, makeup, magazines, the cinema and dancing.[99] Modernity for these women was experienced as growing independence, and a consequence of this was their greater visibility, which attracted criticism.

As fashion writer Elizabeth Wilson has argued, one of the reasons that changes in fashion are ridiculed and condemned so promptly by those seeking to maintain the status quo is because, 'dress . . . forces us to recognise that the human body is more than a biological entity. It is an organism in culture, a cultural artefact even, and its own boundaries are unclear.'[100] The fashionable female body in the 1920s and 1930s was without question a cultural artefact. It was 'situated' at the interface of social, economic and cultural inter-relations. Its promotion, articulation and visibility represented, to a significant extent, women and their increasingly complex identities. Mediating between the biological and the socio-cultural, fashion brought women into discourse, establishing a visual dialogue with their everyday experiences. Through a plethora of means, it insinuated itself into their lives.

Women's magazines continued to be a crucial source of fashion information, and new titles complemented those established earlier in the century, including *Woman and Home* (launched 1926), *Good Housekeeping* (launched 1922) and *Britannia* (launched 1928), which became *Britannia and Eve* in 1929. Addressing a largely lower-middle-class market, these were joined in 1932 by *Woman's Own* and in 1937 by *Woman*. At the upper end of the market was *Harper's Bazaar*, begun in 1929. Other magazines for women which were popular between the wars were romance and fiction magazines such as *Red Letter* (1929), *Secrets* (1932), *True Romances* (1934) and *True Story* (1922).[101] Although these were less concerned with the visual display of fashion, information about appropriate or glamorous dress was communicated through the stories and by the illustrations accompanying these.

In the pages of such magazines, ideals of female beauty were continuously mapped out. In *Woman and Home* in December 1926, an article entitled 'Keeping Up Appearances' advised women on those 'fresh little details which make a woman look well groomed'.[102] All of these – among them drinking warmed orange-juice, using vaseline as cuticle cream, and having a massage – were dependent upon available leisure time, which was limited both for those working long hours in a factory and those raising a family. Accompanying the article was a soft-focus photograph of the profile of a young woman's head with cropped, wavy hair. Dark lips and eyelids recalled the use of makeup in early cinema to create a vulnerable form of beauty.

The loves, lives and films of Hollywood and its stars figured regularly in the pages of most women's magazines during the 1920s and 1930s. The coverage included the obvious use of Hollywood visual iconography, but also in-depth informative articles. In 'Hollywood through the Looking Glass', the writer examined the variety of jobs to be found in Hollywood. Alongside the familiar interest in stars, other women essential in creating the Hollywood look were discussed, for example the wardrobe mistress, the still photographer, the researcher and the head of publicity. Unusually, this particular article criticised the 'factory system of standardisation', and it showed women not just as 'stars' but in a range of responsible jobs.[103] More typical of the growing visual influence of Hollywood were advertisements, such as that for 'Tattoo' lipstick in *Vogue* in 1935, which showed a glamorous blonde model stretched out in a bathing suit dreaming of being serenaded on a deserted island, aided by one of 'four ravishing shades' of lipstick.[104] This particular blonde was a direct descendant of the highly artificial star images epitomised by Jean Harlow, with long peroxide-blonde hair, sharply drawn red lips and high, dark eyebrows.

Fashion was at the core of most of these magazines. Advertising a paper pattern service which provided 'two useful dresses to wear beneath our winter coat styles which the amateur will find easy to make', *Britannia and Eve* illustrated winter coats typical of fashions from the early 1930s, with broad shoulders combined with a natural waistline to give a long, slender silhouette.[105] These particular designs marked a change from the dominant tubular styles of the 1920s; instead, both coats and dresses were tailored to fit close to the body by using bias-cutting, yokes and panels. A return to a natural waist was offset by broad, square shoulders to produce a long tapered outline. Quirky little hats and caps were worn asymmetrically to one side over longer, curled and waved hair, creating a softer look. The overall style was self-consciously clever, due to the complexity of the cut, and at the same time playful, with added bows and scarves. Its origins were to be found in the work of Elsa Schiaparelli (1890–1973), who introduced a sense of wit into fashion at the same time as creating a highly contrived 'cut' which manipulated and sculpted the body, and of Madeleine Vionnet (1876–1975). Vionnet's approach complemented that of Schiaparelli, in that she too cut and draped fabric around the body to accentuate its contours. Her particular technique was the bias-cut which, along with tailoring, articulated the fashionable body in the 1930s.[106]

Three years earlier, *Britannia and Eve* had advertised 'corot tailor-mades', which were not just made-to-measure, but also available by instalments. Designs for smart tailored suits ranged in price from 13 shillings 6d to 15 shillings monthly, or 4–5 guineas cash. As John Stevenson has argued, 'For many items credit facilities were becoming more readily available. By 1938 two-thirds of all larger purchases were made using hire-purchase agreements.'[107] Both Mowat and Stevenson, in discussing economic recovery in Britain during the 1930s, pointed to the importance of increasing levels of consumption. Stevenson outlined a number of inter-related factors which contributed to the growth of consumption. These include the decline in the birth rate which resulted in fewer dependents, the loosening of economic controls, technological advances particularly with regard to new materials, modern industrial processes and organisation (the former based partly on electricity, the latter on 'Taylorism'),[108] modern advertising and retailing techniques, and the extensive programme of council and private house building in the 1920s and 1930s, which stimulated the demand for consumer goods.[109] With a sharp eye on the stimulation of new patterns of consumption, and largely inspired by North American practice, department stores began to offer credit and to market their facilities more aggressively to attract customers. Binns department store, for example, organised 85 special LNER (London North Eastern Railways) trains to deliver customers to their Darlington store for Christmas 1935. This brought shoppers from Leeds, Doncaster, Berwick-upon-Tweed, Hawes and Carlisle, and offered a special lunch for those spending more than £2. In the same year, Binns offered hire purchase at an interest rate of 5 per cent over two years, and as a consequence amassed 30,000 family accounts.[110] Binns, which had stores across the Northeast of England, served a population of four million and employed 3500 in four of its main stores.[111]

Women's economic power resided not merely in their status as consumers, but as producers of goods and services. Large numbers of women found jobs in laundries and dry cleaning, hotels and restaurants, and the entertainment and sports industries. Fashion and its associated industries, such as magazines, were strongly tied to these areas of the economy, and obviously benefited from women's increased spending power. As a particularly vital part of the fashion business, magazines such as *Woman and Home* depended on advertising revenue. The graphic style of illustration used for these in the 1920s originated in the work of Paul Iribe and George Lepape, but had become much debased by the mid- to late 1920s. In a cheaper magazine, such as *Woman and Home*, illustration was merely a formula used to describe rather than to evoke a design, as the original illustrations had done. However, the greater attention to detail which was now evident provided women with an informative source for making their own copies of the ubiquitous 1920s look, whilst 'Kut-Eezi' paper patterns offered a cheap alternative for those requiring a little more instruction.

The fashions of the 1920s marked a continuation and simplification of the styles which had emerged both before and during the First World War. The emphasis remained on simple vertical lines and a studied casualness. New materials, such as rayon, and materials not normally found in high fashion, such as jersey, were used for informal cardigans, unstructured jackets, straight and pleated skirts (ankle-length to mid-calf in the mid-1920s, but just below the knee by the end of the decade), wide loose trousers and short dresses with dropped waists. In its *Journal of New Spring and Summer Fashions* from 1924, the remodelled department store James Coxon, of Market Street, Newcastle-upon-Tyne, advertised new fashions typical of the day (Figure 4.8). These included ribbed wool and jersey 'jumper suits' and costumes which were typical of contemporary styles: colours were muted, such as cinnamon and fawn, and almond and putty; fabrics were casual; outlines were elongated and minimal. In contrast, features from August 1929 and Spring 1930 in *Britannia and Eve* depicted the high modernity of late 1920s fashions in the popular illustrative style of the period, with abstracted, sharply delineated faces drawn in side or three-quarter profiles (Figure 4.9). Shoulders were square, figures were long and slim with few curves. Bottoms, hips, stomach and waists were flattened and boyish, although makeup was highly exaggerated and hair was cut short, bobbed or shingled. Day wear was casual and, by 1930, hems were short. These suits and those from Coxon's *Journal* showed the influence of Paris fashion designers Coco Chanel (1883–1971) and Jean Patou (1887–1936), with their

Figure 4.8: Page from the catalogue of James Coxon & Co. Ltd,
Newcastle-upon-Tyne, 1924. Reproduced by permission of
Beamish, the North of England open air museum.

careful simplicity and subtly co-ordinated informality. Attributed to the house
of Redfern, Chantal and Joseph Paquin, the designs depicted in this issue of
Britannia and Eve show young women checking a map during a day out
motoring with a headline 'Fashion takes a new route with Country Coats and
Suits'.[112] The illustrative style, although referring to the innovations of 20 years
earlier, had clearly moved on, mainly by drawing on advertising devices
used in the USA which emphasised leisure and modernity. Significantly, the
feeling for light and shade created in these illustrations and the concern to
combine detail, but at the same time suggest a mood, prefigured the use of
photography, which became more widespread in the 1930s.

By the 1930s, photography offered a much more modern and evocative
method of representing fashion than illustration. In one image it could capture
a number of qualities, some of which were contradictory, and fashion editors
became increasingly susceptible to the opportunities that this afforded.
At the top end of the magazine market, *Vogue* and *Harper's Bazaar* employed
a number of photographers whose work pushed at the boundaries of
established methods of representing fashion. A good example was Martin
Munkasci (1896–1963) who worked for *Harper's Bazaar* in the USA in the
1930s. His background was as a sports photographer in Romania, and as a
consequence he brought to fashion photography a sense of immediacy and

Figure 4.9: 'Fashion takes a new route with Country
Coats and Suits', illustrations from a fashion feature in
Britannia and Eve, August 1929. Authors' copyright.

movement which epitomised the dynamism of modernity. Instead of the frozen
sculptural elegance of many of his contemporaries, Munkasci photographed
models in action. By the end of the 1930s, the influence of his work was
apparent in English *Vogue*. Gordon Lowe Sports advertising depicted a
model standing on rocks by the edge of the sea wearing a printed linen dress
over a matching swimsuit.[113] A sense of movement and spontaneity was
captured with crisp black-and-white photography in a rough, outdoor setting
rather than in a highly manipulated studio environment.

Such an environment was essential, however, for another strand of innovative fashion photography, which was influenced by Hollywood cinema and
the work of surrealist photographers such as Man Ray and Horst P. Horst.
Images suggestive of Hollywood appeared generally in magazine advertising
as early as 1930; for example, an advert for Wills Capston cigarettes in
Britannia and Eve used cinema-style neon to light up the company and
product name against a dark skyline.[114] However, by the mid-1930s photography was increasingly widespread as a means of representing fashion in
women's magazines, and the apotheosis of the Hollywood influence could be
seen in the high fashion magazine *Vogue* and upmarket women's magazines
such as *Harper's Bazaar* and *The Queen*. In addition, motifs drawn from
surrealism were increasingly evident, and in some cases specific poses were
almost directly copied from surrealist photography. An example of this was

the advertisement for 'Celanese' Court Satin in *Vogue* in May 1935 showing
a model in a statuesque, almost Grecian, pose wearing a bias-cut and draped
evening gown which recalled Man Ray's photograph of a Redfern design
illustrated in *Harper's Bazaar*.[115]

In November 1935, *Vogue* included a fashion feature on the actress
Norma Shearer, who was about to embark on a film of *Romeo and Juliet*.
Two accompanying photographs exemplified the influence of surrealism on
fashion photography. Both photographs were strikingly lit to emphasise dark
shadows relieved by narrow shafts of light coming from unexpected sources.
Interior settings, reminiscent of film sets, combined with the image of Shearer
to create a disconcerting juxtaposition which drew on surrealist devices.
Drawing on Freudian ideas, some surrealist artists had used the female
figure as a metaphor for sexual transgression, deviance and disorder in their
work. In a similar way, the image of Norma Shearer, shot as a silhouette with
elaborate back-lighting and poised on a chaise-longue, was disconcerting
(Figure 4.10). Clothed in a wide-skirted velvet dress and a Juliet-style cap,
this representation of the female body, which was articulated within a framework of drama and history, hinted at the risk and danger of adolescent female

Figure 4.10: Fashion feature with Norma Shearer, *Vogue*,
13 November 1935. Reproduced by permission of Condé
Nast Publications Ltd.

sexuality. The visual language of surrealism utilised in such photographs was ideally suited to represent the ambivalence and fear of disorder which accompanied women's changing social roles and identities within the period. This is reinforced as closer scrutiny also points to the influence of Hollywood, and in particular those films from the 1930s which have subsequently been described as 'women's films' such as *Letty Lynton* (1932). Dramatic lighting and striking, often exaggerated costume, were used to signify disruptive feminine identities in films which dealt with 'the woman question'. Transferred to the realm of fashion, these visual codes allowed a juxtaposition of meanings which, like the films, were at once challenging and reaffirming of patriarchal norms. These fashion images exaggerated, parodied and reiterated fixed notions of female beauty and elegance, but at the same time provoked disquiet at the possibility of disordered and transgressive femininities. In the second photograph (Figure 4.11), the languidly posed Norma Shearer dressed in a sheath-like bias-cut gown with skull-cap of feathers and shot in sharp profile and half-light referred to a plethora of cinema images: in this instance the close-fitting cap which obscured that obvious symbol of femininity, long hair; the sexualised pose which sharply delineated the curves

Figure 4.11: Fashion feature with Norma Shearer, *Vogue*, 13 November 1935. Reproduced by permission of Condé Nast Publications Ltd.

of the stomach, breasts and thighs; and the high drama evoked by strong light and shade refer specifically to Katherine Hepburn's spectacular 'Silver Moth' costume in *Christopher Strong*.[116] Hepburn's masculine-style clothes – trousers, pumps and mandarin jacket – in which she dressed on most occasions in the film and in everyday life were symbolic of her independence, both in real life, confronting studio moguls, and imagined in the film. The dominant theme of the film is that of female sexuality outside accepted boundaries, and the tango which she dances with her lover signifies this, whilst the precariousness and fragility of her position is suggested by the stunning moth-like silver coat-gown and extraordinary silver cap. Interestingly, this particular image, which connoted sexual ambiguity and power, yet at the same time hinted at the potentially predatory nature of female sexuality, was referred to in a number of fashion photographs from the mid-1930s, including this one of Norma Shearer.

Complexity and contradiction characterised women's fashion and the popular representations of it evident in a range of media, but particularly in magazines, advertising, illustration and photography in Britain between the wars. In formal terms, 1920s styles were tubular and androgynous, in that they de-emphasised the curvaceous female form and stressed the straight vertical line, whereas from the early to mid-1930s bias-cutting and draping brought a softer, less angular look which hung around the body, delineating its curves and fullness. This difference was particularly acute in dress styles, although it was also discernible in women's suits, which tended to take on a sharp tailored outline in the 1930s, as opposed to a loose, layered look in the 1920s.[117]

The plethora of fashionable styles and women's access to these cut across class boundaries, due to the availability of new shops and magazines, and the popular appeal of the cinema and the dance hall, which gave women unprecedented levels of knowledge and choice. This was particularly the case for young, single women, for whom fashion provided an arena in which they could, in effect, 're-imagine themselves'. This re-imagining might have been limited to a hairstyle or a way of putting on makeup, or it might have extended to a whole new outfit, either shop-bought or home-made. Nevertheless, the arbitrary nature of fashion, and the transience of different femininities were highlighted as never before in these fashions and fashionable looks. Glamour was a popular style which enabled women, particularly young ones, to confront dominant constructions of femininity with a knowing disrespect. In this context, the red-lipped, silk-stockinged, young woman attacked by Orwell and Priestley were not merely symbols of an unwelcome 'feminine' modernity, but also prescient of the rejection of an essentially patriarchal notion of femininity – one which was unchanging and universal. Due to its symbiotic relationship with the body, fashion gave women an immediate and 'knowable' visual means to signal the paradoxes of being 'female'. In analysing the fashionable styles worn by women between the wars, it is significant how many of these called into question accepted and conventional ways of shaping and covering the body, particularly by either undermining heterosexual gendered identities and minimising sexual difference (more typical of the 1920s) or by exaggerating them (a characteristic of the 1930s). Fashion in the inter-war years did not clothe a neutral body, it brought it into discourse, and the dominant discourses which related to women were constituted around sex, the sex war, sexual freedom, sexual promiscuity and the anxieties which this provoked. In this respect, the breasts, hips, legs, stomach, back, face and waist were emphasised at one stage or another during the 1920s and 1930s. Gaunt, dramatic makeup, backless gowns, androgynous tubular shifts, figure-hugging bias-cuts, square-shouldered jackets and nipped-in waists all served to expose the sexualised body.

Modernity provided a critical context for this as women's engagement with clothing production, fashion retailing and consumption opened up new spaces for women. It linked women to modern life and contemporary culture. It drew them into the cultural arena in a very public way as they aspired to styles which referred to Hollywood films and lifestyles in which women acted out alternative roles to the ones for which most of them were destined. In fact it was the whole paraphernalia of fashion which contributed to this sense of modernity, and pointed to the possibility of change: the window-shopping, the magazines and sales leaflets, and the physical experience of the shops themselves, modernised, technological, and streamlined. The glamour of Hollywood and the cosmopolitanism of fashions which had originated in Paris, London or New York, but were available in cheaper versions across Britain, brought the internationalism of modernity to the private home.

Women's involvement with fashion, as producers and consumers, enabled them to experience modernity at first hand. At the same time, it provided a vehicle for them to explore the meaning of femininity within the changing context of British social, economic and cultural life between the wars. Modernity in its many guises undermined established identities, bringing new industrial processes and systems, new retailing and marketing techniques, and new visual icons to Britain. Women and fashion had a pivotal role in this: as workers and producers they were employed in the new industries and the service sector. They took on work deemed 'feminine' as a consequence of essentialist notions of sexual difference and the vestiges of the sexual division of labour, and due to capitalist economics, as cheap semi-skilled labour. As consumers, women played a large part in stimulating new shopping facilities and the design and manufacture of a plethora of lower-priced, available, fashionable goods. In the new industries and shops, in making, buying and wearing fashionable clothes, and in creating new visual representations of femininity, women were engaged in constructing new identities within the context of British social, economic and cultural life. In this, they participated in and indeed helped to precipitate a modernity based on their needs and experiences – a 'feminine modernity' which called into question notions of women's place within society and struck at the heart of patriarchal power.

NOTES ON CHAPTER 4

1   Judy Giles, '"Playing Hard to Get": Working-class Women, Sexuality and Respectability in Britain, 1918–1940', in *Women's History Review*, vol. 3, no 1 (1994), p.241.

2   Charles L. Mowat, *Britain Between the Wars* (Cambridge, Methuen, 1987), p.212.

3   Mowat, *Britain Between the Wars*, p.212.

4   *Hidden From History* (London, Pluto Press, 1973), p.125.

5   Sheila Rowbotham, *Hidden from, History*, p.126.

6   Sally Alexander, 'Becoming a woman in London in the 1920s and 1930s', in Sally Alexander, *Becoming a Woman and Other Essays in 19th and 20th Century Feminist History* (London, Virago, 1994), pp.203–24.

7   Winifred Holtby, *Women and a Changing Civilisation* (London, John Lane, 1934), p.119.

8   Susan Kingsley Kent, *Making Peace: The Reconstruction of Gender in Interwar Britain* (Princeton, Princeton University Press, 1993), p.100.

9   For more detail see: Alexander, *Becoming A Woman*, Johanna Alberti, 'The Turn of the Tide: Sexuality and Politics, 1928–1931' *Women's History Review*, vol. 3, no 2, 1994, pp.169–90; Deirdre Beddoe, *Back to Home and Duty: Women Between the Wars, 1918–1939* (London, Pandora, 1989); Giles, '"Playing Hard to Get"', pp.239–55; Hilda Kean, 'Searching for the Past in Present Defeat: The Construction of Historical and Political Identity in British Feminism in the 1920s and 1930s', *Women's History Review*, vol. 3, no 1 (1994), pp.59–80; Kingsley Kent, *Making Peace*; Martin Pugh, *Women and The Women's Movement in Britain 1914–1959*, (London, Macmillan, 1992); Sheila Rowbotham, *A New World For Women: Stella Browne – Socialist Feminist* (London, Pluto Press, 1978).

10   Beddoe, *Back to Home and Duty*, p.7.

11   Giles, '"Playing Hard to Get"', p.241.

12   Ibid.

13   Alison Light, *Forever England: Femininity, Literature and Conservatism Between the Wars* (London, Routledge, 1991), p.10.

14   Alexander, *Becoming A Woman*, p.245.

15   Ibid., p.246.

16   George Orwell, *Coming Up for Air* (London, Penguin, 1990; first published 1939), p.9.

17   George Orwell, 'England Your England', in *Inside the Whale and Other Essays* (London, Penguin, 2001), pp.88–9.

18   For example, the North East Coast Exhibition, staged in the centre of Newcastle-upon-Tyne and opened on 14 May 1929 by the Prince of Wales, just a few months after the Wall Street crash propelled Tyneside along with the rest of Britain into economic depression, was organised to ensure that the area would not experience trade depression and unemployment of the kind from which it seemed to be emerging. It aimed to revive trade in the Northeast and develop new industries at a time when the traditional heavy industries of coal-mining, shipbuilding and engineering still faced difficulties stemming from the loss of markets during the First World War. A great success, the exhibition attracted nearly 4 million visitors.

19   Alexander, *Becoming A Woman*, p.248.

20   Giles, '"Playing Hard to Get"', p.241.

21   Alexander, *Becoming A Woman*, p.264.

22   Alberti, 'The Turn of the Tide', p.179.

23   Advert, *Britannia and Eve*, June 1929, p.16.

24   Alexander, *Becoming A Woman*, p.262.

25   Frederick Taylor's methods of scientific management began to be more widely understood and implemented in Britain in the 1920s and 1930s. These were complemented by an increased awareness and knowledge of American sales and marketing techniques, which radically altered the image and approach of companies such as Marks & Spencer. See Goronwy Rees, *St Michael: A History of Marks & Spencer* (London, Weidenfeld and Nicholson), 1969.

26   From Eric Leeds, *No Man's Land: Combat and Identity in World War 1*, quoted by Kingsley Kent, *Making Peace*, p.99.

27   Kingsley Kent, *Making Peace*, p.113.

28   Holtby, *Women and a Changing Civilisation*, p.7.

29   See Pugh, *Women and the Women's Movement*, Beddoe, *Back to Home and Duty* and Kingsley Kent, *Making Peace* for more details regarding the political and tactical differences within inter-war feminism.

30   Kingsley Kent, *Making Peace*, p.117.

31   Ibid., p.107.

32   Ibid.

33   Rowbotham, *Hidden from History*, p.143.

34   Marie Stopes, *Married Love* (A.C. Fifield, 1918).

35   Cate Haste, *Rules of Desire: Sex in Britain, World War 1 to the Present* (London, Chatto and Windus, 1992), p.61.

36   Radclyffe Hall, *The Well of Loneliness* (London, Cape, 1928).

37   Marie Stopes, *Married Love* (A.C. Fifield, 1918).

38   Beddoe, *Back to Home and Duty*, pp.106–7. According to Haste in *Rules of Desire*, p.63, Marie Stopes's first clinic doubled its attendance each year

from 518 women in 1921 to 2368 in 1923. She opened 12 more clinics in largely working-class areas around Britain by 1930.

39   Margery Spring Rice, *Working-class Wives* (London, Virago, 1981), p.56.
40   See Rowbotham, *A New World For Women*. In this, Rowbotham describes a number of meetings that Stella Browne addressed in the Rhondda in South Wales on birth control. Two of the meetings were women only. At these 'every foot of space was packed and women mostly with babies…stood five deep in rows behind the chairs' (p.31). On another tour, an older woman came up to her and announced that birth control was too late for her, but not for her daughters (p.31).
41   Alexander, *Becoming a Woman*, p.263.
42   Pugh, *Women and The Women's Movement in Britain 1914–1959*, p.253–4.
43   Elizabeth Roberts, *A Woman's Place: An Oral History of Working-class Women 1890–1940* (Oxford, Blackwell, 1984), pp.14–16.
44   A. Pearl Jephcott, *Girls Growing Up* (London, Faber and Faber, 1942), p.139.
45   Ibid., p.139.
46   Holtby, *Women and a Changing Civilisation*, p.121.
47   See for example Theodor Adorno, 'On Popular Music', in John Storey, *Cultural Theory and Popular Culture: A Reader* (Hemel Hempstead, Harvester Wheatsheaf, 1994), pp.202–3.
48   Holtby, *Women and a Changing Civilisation*, p.118.
49   Mica Nava and Alan O'Shea, *Modern Times: Reflections on a Century of English Modernity* (London, Routledge, 1996), p.63.
50   Ibid.
51   Alberti, 'The Turn of the Tide', p.184.
52   Jephcott, *Girls Growing Up*, p.36.
53   Ibid., pp.36–7.
54   Ibid., p.38.
55   See Jeffrey Richards, *The Age of the Dream Palace: Cinema and Society in Britain 1930–1939* (London, Routledge & Kegan Paul, 1984).
56   Jackie Stacey, *Star Gazing: Hollywood Cinema and Female Spectatorship* (London, Routledge, 1994), pp.57–8
57   Giles, '"Playing Hard to Get"', p.252.
58   Jephcott, *Girls Growing Up*, p.118
59   Ibid.
60   Jephcott, *Girls Growing Up*, p.118.
61   Giles, '"Playing Hard to Get"', p.264.
62   Charlotte Herzog and Jane Gaines, '"Puffed Sleeves Before Tea-time": Joan Crawford, Adrian and Women Audiences', in Christine Gledhill, *Stardom: Industry of Desire* (London, Routledge, 1991).
63   See Herzog and Gaines essay, ibid., for details of the ways in which a particular dress worn by Joan Crawford in *Letty Lynton* (1932) was popularised by the fashion industry.

64   Annette Kuhn, *Women's Pictures: Feminism and Cinema* (London, Routledge, 1982), p.89.

65   Jephcott, *Girls Growing Up*, p.119.

66   Richards, *The Age of the Dream Palace*, p.15.

67   Richards, *The Age of the Dream Palace*, p.13.

68   Stacey, *Star Gazing*, p.99.

69   Ibid., p.97.

70   Adrian Forty, *Objects of Desire: Design and Society 1750–1980* (London, Thames and Hudson, 1986), Ch. 5.

71   Alexander, *Becoming A Woman*, p.266.

72   See Lynne Walker, 'Vistas of Pleasure: Women Consumers of Urban Space in the West End of London 1850–1900', in Clarissa Campbell Orr (ed.), *Women in the Victorian Art World* (Manchester, Manchester University Press, 1995).

73   William Lancaster, *The History of the Department Store* (Leicester, Leicester University Press, 1995).

74   Gareth Jones, *Workers at Play: A Social and Economic History of Leisure 1918–1939* (London, Routledge & Kegan Paul, 1986).

75   Jephcott, *Girls Growing Up*, p.123.

76   For a fuller discussion of the relationships between African-American jazz and blues and modernity, see Paul Gilroy, *The Black Atlantic Modernity and Double Consciousness* (London, Verso, 1993).

77   Jephcott, *Girls Growing Up*, pp.124–5.

78   'Nippy: The story of her day', *Picture Post*, 4 March 1939, pp.29–34.

79   Ibid., pp.33–4.

80   Department stores saw a two- or threefold increase, and multiples a four-fold increase. Between 1926 and 1940, Marks & Spencer opened or rebuilt 218 stores, and by 1939 the company had 234 stores across Britain. See Rees, *St Michael*.

81   Lancaster, *The History of the Department Store*.

82   See Erika D. Rappaport, '"A New Era of Shopping": The promotion of Women's Pleasure in London's West End, 1901–1914', in Leo Charney and Vanessa R. Schwartz (eds), *Cinema and the Invention of Modern Life* (Berkeley, California, University of California Press, 1995), pp.130–55.

83   See Barbara Burman, *The Culture of Sewing: Gender, Consumption and Home Dressmaking* (Oxford, Berg, 1999).

84   My aunt, Betty Foster, was taught to knit and sew by the lady's maid when she was in service in the 1940s. See Cheryl Buckley, 'On the Margins: Theorizing the History and Significance of Making and Designing Clothes at Home', *Journal of Design History*, vol. 11, no 2, pp.157–71. This essay is reprinted in Burman, *The Culture of Sewing*, 1999.

85   Ibid.

86   See Cheryl Buckley, 'Modernity, Femininity and Regional Identity: Women and Fashion in the North East of England, 1914–1940' in Thomas, E.

Faulkner, *Northumbrian Panorama: Studies in the History and Culture of North East England* (London, Octavian Press, 1996).

87   James B. Jefferys has argued that the market share of the multiple or variety chain store type of firm was estimated to have risen from negligible proportions in 1920 (well under 3 per cent) to nearly 20 per cent in 1938. See James B. Jefferys, *Retail Trading in Britain 1850–1950* (Cambridge, Cambridge University Press, 1954), pp.69–70.

88   See Barbara Drake, *Women in Trade Unions* (London, Virago, 1984).

89   Ibid., p.141.

90   Ibid., Table II: Analysis of principal trade unions.

91   Elizabeth Wilson, *Adorned in Dreams* (London, Virago, 1985), p.79.

92   Both Burton and Prices Tailors Ltd expanded during the depression years. By 1935, Burtons had over 400 branches, and Prices over 250. See Jefferys, *Retail Trading in Britain*, p.305; Frank Mort, *Cultures of Consumption, Masculinities and Social Space in Late Twentieth-century Britain* (London, Routledge, 1996), pp.134–45.

93   Jephcott, *Girls Growing Up*, p.84.

94   Susan Porter Benson, *Counter Cultures: Saleswomen, Managers and Customers in American Department Stores, 1890–1940* (Chicago, University of Illinois Press, Urbana and Chicago, 1988), p.5.

95   Ibid., p.111.

96   There is a misplaced assumption that working-class women generally did not return to domestic service after the First World War. This was not the case. In 1921, 33 per cent of all working women were employed in domestic service, and in 1931 this had risen to 35 per cent. See Christina Hardyment, *From Mangle to Microwave: The Mechanisation of Household Work* (London, Polity Press, 1988.)

97   One such woman was Elizabeth Clennell. She was born in 1896 and brought up in Newcastle-upon-Tyne, the daughter of a brickworks manager. The eldest of three children, she attended a secretarial college in Newcastle and gained employment in the city in various offices, including Shell, for whom she worked as a shorthand typist. Interview with Mavis Robinson, 24 August 1993.

98   Beddoe, *Back to Home and Duty*, p.57.

99   These views are critically discussed by Sally Alexander, who aimed to re-evaluate the experiences of working-class women in London, whose aspirations were viewed by J.B. Priestley and G. Orwell as indicative of the 'feminisation' of everyday life. They implied that this process of 'feminisation' contributed to the undermining of authentic working-class culture and society which, significantly, originated in the experiences of skilled male industrial workers. The aspirations of these young women, who were working in the service sector and in the new light industries, were represented as being somewhat immoral in the context of rising male unemployment in the traditional heavy industries. Significantly, these

left-wing writers celebrated the implicit masculinity of the traditional industries of shipbuilding, coal-mining, engineering etc, and its ensuing culture. Their claims to be chroniclers of working-class experiences needs to be seen within the context of their neglect of women from the working class, who sought paid employment and independent lives, and their contempt for the different, more modern, cultural and social aspirations of these women.

100 Wilson, *Adorned in Dreams*, p.2.

101 Janice Winship, *Inside Women's Magazines* (London, Pandora, 1987), p.166.

102 *Woman and Home*, December 1926, p.37.

103 *Britannia and Eve*, October 1929, pp.30–33.

104 *Vogue*, 13 November 1935, p.17.

105 *Britannia and Eve*, November 1933, pp.70–71.

106 For an interesting discussion of the work of Coco Chanel, Elsa Schiaparelli and Madeleine Vionnet, see Caroline Evans and Minna Thornton, *Women and Fashion: A New Look* (London, Quartet, 1989), Ch. 6.

107 John Stevenson, *British Society 1914–45* (London, Pelican, 1984), p.113. See also Mowat, *Britain Between the Wars* for discussion of economic issues, particularly regarding consumption between the wars.

108 Taylorism refers to the system of scientific management developed by the American Frederick W. Taylor in the early years of the twentieth century and outlined in his book, *The Principles of Scientific Management* (1911). It aimed to make factory organisation more rational and cost-effective in terms of human time and industrial planning.

109 Stevenson, *British Society*, p.111–14.

110 For further information on Binns, see Michael Moss and Alison Turton, *A Legend of Retailing... House of Fraser* (London, Weidenfield & Nicholson, 1989). See also the House of Fraser archives, Business Records Archive, Glasgow University.

111 New stores opened in Darlington in 1922; Middlesbrough in 1925; West Hartlepool in 1926; South Shields in 1927; Newcastle in 1929.

112 The house of Redfern was established in 1841, and closed in the late 1920s. See Colin McDowell, *Directory of Twentieth Century Fashion*, (London, Muller, 1974). *Britannia and Eve*, August 1929, pp.66–7.

113 See advertisement for Gordon Lowe Sports in *Vogue*, 28 April 1937, p.34.

114 *Britannia and Eve*, June 1930, p.127.

115 *Vogue*, 1 May 1935, p.167.

116 *Vogue*, 13 November 1935.

117 See, for example, Lou Taylor and Elizabeth Wilson, *Through the Looking Glass: A History of Dress from 1860 to the Present Day* (London, BBC, 1989) and Wilson, *Adorned in Dreams*, 1985.

5 'Doon the Toon': Young Women, Fashion and Sexuality

This chapter explores the changing relationship between young women, fashion, sexuality and identity through the period of post-modernity, between the 1960s and the beginning of the twenty-first century. Using Newcastle-upon-Tyne as a site for a particular contemporary study, it will examine issues of class and regionality in the context of wider concerns about female representation in fashion and the popular media.

My own interest in fashion evolved as I was growing up in the 1960s. The relative austerity of my 1950s childhood heightened the sense of excitement to be found for me in entering my teens in a newly expanding world of consumption. My mother, through her marriage to my father, had been recently established in the lower-middle class after a working-class upbringing, and saw fashion as an arena of aspiration in which young women could define themselves. I was tutored in differentiating between clothes that were 'classy' and 'common', learning the unacceptability of such combinations as American tan tights and white shoes. In my early teens, on evenings when my father went out with his friends, my mother and I would pore over fashion pages in the popular magazines *Woman* and *Woman's Own* as I took a break from my homework. The world of fashion was a frivolous contrast to the constant pressures of school work to which girls in the 'baby-boomer' generation were being increasingly subjected in the post-war world of expanding opportunity. My love of fashion was part of the tension between the achieving me and the traditionally feminine me, the me that would be the first woman in my family to enter higher education and the me that identified with my housewife mother and her engagement with the rules of style and good taste.

For much of the period of my teens, I lived in a state of constant frustration that the 'trendy' clothes that I saw in the magazine *Honey*[1] or on the television programme *Ready Steady Go*[2] were unavailable in provincial

Sunderland, where I grew up, or even in Newcastle, the nearest major city. I rejected the blandishments of my mother to eat more home-cooked food as I began to imitate the increasingly thin role models with which young women were confronted in the fashion media. By the end of the 1960s, I had left home and was at university in Newcastle, where I studied Fine Art. Freed from parental restriction, I took great pleasure in travelling regularly to London, where I bought clothes with the money that I had saved from my grant by dint of rigorous dieting. My first destination was the Biba Emporium on Kensington High Street, which seemed an exciting world away from the then provincial drabness of the Northeast of England, and I clearly remember the sense of fevered anticipation followed by delight in the visual aesthetic of the shop and the ever-changing subtleties of the fashion on display. Anxieties lay in the changing rooms, however, where all we skinny size eights and tens would scrutinise each other for any physical imperfection, any iota of excess flesh. I was motivated then by the competition to be highly fashionable, and to be thin, and would devour copies of *Vogue* and French *Elle* looking for new ideas and identities.

My lower-middle-class background provided me with few social advantages, but my ability to read fashion and place myself 'ahead of the game' gave me an edge that felt powerful in a world in which as a young woman I still felt essentially powerless. The changing fashion system allowed young people like myself to reinvent ourselves in terms of social status through the ever-changing subtleties of fashion, and for a moment enjoy the possibility of uniqueness and difference that the dynamic popular market allowed the newly enfranchised consumer. Such distinction could be achieved quite cheaply, but it was a metropolitan construct; you had to travel to London, and know where to shop to buy it. It required dedication, a serious commitment to the pursuit of 'cool' and an ultra-slim body. Whatever else I did in that period, I felt that I did fashion best. It was an arena in which I felt confident. However confused I may have been about my role in the world, on the outside I looked in control, totally of the moment.

I still have some clothes from that period at home, tiny little dresses and jackets that look now like a child's clothes, and seem part of a strange world, so long ago when that desire for 'the Look' often dominated my life and reduced my world to a pursuit of an ever-illusive ideal of self. My wedding outfit, Ossie Clark dress and Biba shoes, represented a climactic moment in my pursuit of fashionability. I was just twenty, too young to be married, but standing outside my local church in Sunderland I represented a triumph of style over good sense (Figure 5.1). The supposedly sexually liberated 1960s had little impact on myself and many other young women in the provinces who jumped into early marriages in a desire for independence and status. The caché of an engagement ring still outweighed the significance of a degree

Figure 5.1: Hilary Fawcett married in Ossie Clark dress, Sunderland, August 1970. Own collection.

diploma for many of us in a world that still carried within it the values of my mother's generation, despite the rapidly expanding opportunities available to young women. My sophisticated and at times sexually provocative appearance was at odds with the reality of my experience of femininity.

It was in the mid- to late 1970s that I began to understand something of the significance of fashion for women, and the ways in which femininity was commodified within its processes. I had already begun to be aware of the pressures inherent in the constant pursuit of the perfect body, and the energy-absorbing nature of the techniques of femininity. I had difficulty integrating the airbrushed images of the women that surrounded me in magazines and on billboards with the experience of child-rearing, domestic life and professional ambition. So-called second-wave feminism allowed me to examine the problems for women inherent in the existing fashion system, with its emphasis on slimness, and that, along with child-bearing, made me see and experience my own body differently. I began to enjoy eating again, and identified with women like those that I had admired as a young girl who were successful in ways other than in their control over their bodies and their appearance. This is not to say that I ceased to experience the conflicts inherent for women in a culture dominated by objectified images of femininity, but it gave me a distance from which I could negotiate for myself issues of image and identity.

In 1971, in *The Female Eunuch*, Germaine Greer wrote:

> Women are so brainwashed about the physical image that they should have that, despite popular fiction on the point, they rarely dress with éclat. They are often apologetic about their bodies, considered in relation to that plastic object of desire whose image is radiated through the media.[3]

This engagement with issues of fashion and female representation continued as a theme in popular and academic feminism throughout the 1970s and into the 1980s. A range of positions, from the vehemently anti-fashion to a more accommodating, if critical, standpoint, were represented by the different feminist identities that operated in the period. Radical feminists, and indeed some of their more liberal 'sisters', abandoned cosmetics and adopted either dungarees and 'earth shoes' or other types of dress, which in their eclecticism removed them from the terrain of mainstream fashion. The 'politics of appearance' were engaged with across the media, in popular magazines such as *Honey* and *Cosmopolitan* as well as in newspapers, both broadsheet and tabloid. The feminist magazine *Spare Rib* frequently addressed issues concerning fashion and female imagery in the early 1970s, with articles such as Lisa Tickner's 'Why not slip into something a little more comfortable?' which recounted the historical relationship between feminism and fashion, and challenged women to question the constraints of conventional female dress.[4] Another was Laura Mulvey's article 'You don't know what is happening, do you Mr Jones?', an early attempt at feminist cultural criticism, using psychoanalysis as a tool to examine dominant female imagery in art and popular culture.[5]

There was a return to a highly glamorous female identity in some mainstream fashion sites in the late 1960s and early 1970s and this continued throughout the decade with examples of soft-focus and airbrushed images in fashion photography and advertising campaigns, such as that of Revlon, which alluded to the photographic techniques developed in soft pornography in the 1960s. By the end of the decade, Jane Fonda had opened her first workout studio in Los Angeles, thus marking the beginning of a period in which the body was to become a site of even more intensive focus. However, it is possible, when looking at copies of *Vogue* in the late 1970s, to identify a range of options in relation to women's fashion that allowed for an engagement with a more complex range of identities than had been the case earlier in the decade.[6] Even Gianni Versace, who was to be the king of body-clinging lycra in the 1980s, was designing for the label Jenny, and producing unstructured layered clothes wearable by a range of shapes and age groups.[7]

Familiar high-street chains that are now identified with a very narrow main-stream market, such as French Connection, were producing comfortable and lively fashion for younger women using cotton and other natural fibres.[8] Laura Ashley provided a particular identity for 1970s earth mothers, in presenting a ruralist aesthetic in cotton that could go through the hot wash. At the same time in the wider media, the image of Diane Keaton in Woody Allen's film *Annie Hall*, with her eclectic layered clothing produced a new kind of Hollywood construct in terms of femininity, another pointer to the possibilities of more complex and interesting choices than the stereotypical *Charlie's Angels* image that dominated certain areas of the media.

In Britain in the later 1970s, punk provided some young women with a truly radical visual identity. The black clothing, often incorporating fetish wear, combined with obviously dyed spiked hair and ghastly makeup was antithetical to the images of the Christie Brinkley version of 'natural femininity' dominating mainstream fashion magazines. Vivienne Westwood, whose role in the development of punk was contentious but whose designs represented a synthesis of the style, declaimed 'if you don't want to attract a chauvinist pig, then you've got to show that you've got something going for you, if you're a woman you're in control of things – that's to do with sex'.[9] Caroline Evans and Minna Thornton, in their book *Women and Fashion*, discussed the way in which within punk women

> by their juxtapositions and appropriations, did not so much resolve contra-dictions as raise them as issues. They were women but appeared not to want to be 'feminine'; they were tarty but they were not tarts; their appearance had a disquieting overtone of violence. In repudiating good taste, classiness and naturalness they were a shock to fashion orthodoxy and to other women.[10]

Punk represented an idiom for young women charged with the momentum of second-wave feminism yet rejective of puritanical constraints and the literal-ness of established modes of anti-fashion. In the complex language of punk, with its dissonant signifiers, there was an attempt to create a visual syntax that interrogated dominant tropes of heterosexuality, as represented in female clothing, and that should have provided an opportunity for the beginning of a real exploration of the relationship between female appearance and desire and the development of a more female-centred fashion system.

It was a missed opportunity. The energy of post-punk and the influence of Japanese designers such as Rei Kawakubo and Issey Miyake at the beginning of the 1980s was soon dissipated, and after a flurry of inventiveness and engagement with issues of gender and identity, British fashion was reappro-priated within the dominant axis of mainstream capitalism. There has been little to challenge radically the hegemonic consensus around fashion and gender since that point. In looking at dominant trends in young women's fashion now, and at the popular media connected to it, I am struck by its formulaic predictability and the ever-escalating pressure on girls to conform to images of highly stereotypical femininity.

In the mid-1980s, Elizabeth Wilson identified the pleasures and possible empowerment, as well as the problems, for women within fashion. Her book *Adorned in Dreams* represented the identification of fashion as a subject for serious academic work, alongside studies of women in popular visual culture by writers such as Judith Williamson,[11] Rosalind Coward,[12] Jane Root[13] and Janice Winship.[14] It contributed to what seemed to be the beginning of a serious and ongoing feminist debate around the subject. However, at the same moment, outside the academic milieu, in the area of dominant cultural representation and femininity, changes were taking place that have had a lasting effect on the relationship between women and fashion, and to which, I would argue, feminists have subsequently failed to make an appropriate response.

The consumer culture of the 1980s was one in which there was a dramatic escalation and expansion in fashion markets, and in the attendant cultures of advertising and magazines. The so-called 'designer decade' began with the success of post-punk and Japanese design, both of which challenged gendered stereotypes by offering alternative approaches to the structure of clothing and the style of femininity. The cultural status of fashion increased, and British design regained the reputation that it had in the 1960s for innovation. In their book *Women and Fashion: A New Look,* published in 1989, Caroline Evans and Minna Thornton claimed that 'The feminist rejection of fashion was itself an experiment and it is now possible to imagine ways to direct that experiment into fashion'.[15] However, it could be argued that Japanese designers such as Rei Kawakubo and the British Vivienne Westwood had already engaged with such experimentation in work that was executed in the late 1970s and early 1980s, and that since the mid-1980s there has been relatively little evidence of any significant or radical engagement with the politics of dress in relation to gender.

As early as 1985 there began to be a definitive shift back to a more conventionally feminine look in women's clothes, and an ever-increasing emphasis on the body in fashion after a number of years in which some designers had been concerned with gender and the structure of clothing in more abstract and creative ways. One explanation is that the cultural impact of the AIDS epidemic resulted in a moral panic in which sexual activity was displaced by display, resulting in the spectacularisation of the body within the visual media. It is noticeable too that, as in the late nineteenth century, in periods in which there are exaggerated anxieties about homosexuality, gender stereotyping appears more pronounced, in a way that gives further definition to sexual difference.

Jean-Paul Gaultier became successful in this period, and his early designs played with issues of power and sexuality with an irony borrowed from punk. His work was amusing and stylish, and his skirt for men was a real attempt to challenge the masculine retreat to the safety of Armani after a decade or more of 'gender bending'. However, his designs for women became more problematic as the decade progressed, and his attempts to reconcile glamour with the subversive in relation to female sexuality failed to challenge the march of Versace and Lagerfeld. It is in his professional relationship with Madonna that Gaultier's designs have had the most lasting cultural significance. The status of Madonna as post-modernist icon has been widely debated, and I do not intend to revisit this material in great detail, but I do believe that her image and attitude in the late 1980s represented a defining moment in the development of a cultural identity for young women in the subsequent period, and therefore had a significant impact in the direction of fashion for this age group.

Dressed by Gaultier, Madonna in the late 1980s confronted negative and oppressive representations of femininity and female sexuality in Western culture by using a visual language that alluded to the conventions of female sexual objectification but placed them in a different context. The famous pink satin corset with pointed and stitched bra cups designed by Gaultier was sensational in its impact, and was part of the apparatus by which Madonna, performing in a massive media spotlight, attempted to redefine contemporary femininity in relation to sexuality and power. Whereas Vivienne Westwood's work in challenging the orthodoxies of female appearance in the early days of punk had smashed the stereotype by using strongly conflicting signifiers, this construct by Madonna, via Gaultier, was one of a stylised but essentially conventional glamour. The pointed breasts of the corset have aggressive connotations, but the lasting impression of the image is of the manicured, svelte, lipsticked Madonna dressed in pink satin. Taken out of the context of her video performances, with their references to polymorphous perversity and assertions of sexual power, her image when reduced to a two-dimensional format was readily reappropriated by the dominant culture, and ultimately endorsed the very values that Madonna claimed to question.

While the need for the subject of female sexuality to be opened in public space was undeniable in her approach to this issue, Madonna proved a contentious icon for feminists. In a 1993 book, *The Madonna Connection*, editor Cathy Schwichtenberg brought together a range of theoretical positions from within feminism. Susan Bordo, Roseann M. Mandzuik and E. Ann Kaplan represented a position broadly critical of the positioning of Madonna as postmodernist icon, with Mandzuik concluding that the post-modern feminism essentially represented the privileging 'of the discourse of style'[16] over political intervention. Other contributors, such as Schwichtenberg herself, were committed to identifying Madonna as representing the politics of resistance within post-modern culture. This material, and the majority of work done by other writers concerned with Madonna's imagery and texts, was written before the longer-term implications of her approach to the representation of female sexuality and identity had been observed.

Within popular American feminism, writers Naomi Wolf[17] and Susan Faludi,[18] who both produced bestselling books in the early 1990s scrutinising the cultures of beauty and fashion, failed to identify the role of Madonna in ultimately colluding in the processes with which they were concerned. When Faludi, in the chapter 'Dressing the Dolls' in *Backlash*, describes the strategies of American fashion markets in creating new ultra-feminine clothing to support failing markets she ignores the significance of Madonna's Cindy-Sherman inspired reinventions of self as relating to this new buoyancy in fashion markets. In her various glamorous personae, from Marilyn Monroe to Marlene Dietrich, I would argue that Madonna was not only reinforcing a spectacularisation of femininity, but also a fragmentation of identity for women that contributed to the process by which 'The subject is required literally to split itself into diverse, often incongruous personae, don mutually exclusive masks entailing predetermined modes of activity, embrace an ethos of unrelieved impermanence'.[19]

Camille Paglia, writing in the early 1990s, endorsed Madonna's self-perception that she was subverting the passive female sexual stereotype and promoted her as a new feminist ideal: 'Madonna taught women how to be fully female and sexual while still exercising control over their lives'.[20] These words represent the essence of popular post-feminist rhetoric, and combine an essentialist position on femininity with a failure to engage with wider issues of class and identity. Paglia's elevation by the American media and parts of the academy to the heights of foremost feminist intellectual was analogous to the lionising of Madonna as feminist icon, in that both women failed to consider the subtleties and complexities of consumer culture in relation to the construction of identity. Rosi Braidotti has argued that in order to create a space for identification of our own desires: 'like Madonna we must visit the sites of assumed essentialism and work through them'.[21] However, Roseann Mandzuik's claim that 'when feminism accepts the dehistoricizing tendency of the post-modern, it loses its specificity as a discourse different from and in opposition to the historicised power of patriarchal narratives'[22] identifies the problems inherent in trying to effect political change from a position so central to mass consumer culture.

The relationship between women's appearance, their bodies, clothes and cosmetics and their sexuality is extant. Madonna, corseted by Gaultier, challenged what she identified as the puritanical approach of second-wave feminism in order to redefine female desire as active yet existing within the tropes of conventional heterosexual representation. I would argue that even the representation of lesbian sexuality in *Justify my Love* is, as Ann Kaplan suggests, masking 'the lesbian scene or making it a spectacle for the male gaze'.[23] Susan Bordo states, 'We are surrounded by homogenising and normalising images – images whose content is far from arbitrary but instead suffused with the dominance of gendered, racial, class and other cultural iconography'.[24] In the context of this proposition, the intended irony of Madonna's homage to the female erotic is lost in the processes of marketing and consumption within high capitalism. The power of the imagery is subsumed into a popular culture dominated by conventionally sexualised images of women.

Obviously Madonna represents only a part of the shift to the heightened femininity in fashion and female iconography which is to be found in the 1990s. Her success ran concurrently with that of 'the supermodel' and a beauty culture in which plastic surgery began to challenge aerobics as the body discipline of choice for media celebrities. Global capitalism in this period threw out ever-more-glamorous and eroticised images of women in fashion, advertising and across the popular media. As Steven Connor has observed, 'the fashion industry, greedy as it is for new and diverse images, functions as part of an economy which depends more and more on forms of publicity as commodity, upon "publicity" and less and less on the exchange of actual goods and services'.[25]

Madonna's strategy in relation to the representation of female sexuality and power has contributed to the silencing of any real dissent by women of her generation and younger, who were won over by her rhetoric and that of her apologists. It has become almost unacceptable for women to question the conventional fashion processes, as to do so implies an attachment to a past that is no longer considered relevant to modern women. 'New feminists' or 'post-feminists', such as Natasha Walter, have followed Paglia and younger American writers in marginalising old feminist concerns and shifting the debates elsewhere at the same time as many feminists in the academy have been largely concerned with the increasingly arcane theoretical approaches to issues of female sexuality and power, and have failed to connect with a generation that has been effectively depoliticised.

Where does this leave young women at the turn of the twenty-first century? I have chosen to examine the experience of young women as consumers of fashion in the city of Newcastle-upon-Tyne in the context of regionality and class as well as wider issues of sexuality, femininity and identity. Newcastle has gained an international reputation as a 'party city' in the past ten or more years. The old image of industrial dreariness has given way to a much more European and stylish identity of exciting new architecture and innovative cultural enterprise. Once a gastronomic desert, the city is now

thronged with restaurants and cafes offering a wide range of food in sur-
roundings that would not look out of place in London or Barcelona. Yet
despite all these developments Newcastle remains a city tied to its past in terms
of its regional identity, sitting as it does in the midst of the now decaying
remnants of what was a massively productive industrial landscape.

My experience of the city in the 1960s as somewhere that offered little
in terms of fashion retailing no longer holds. The immediate incorporation
of the designer look into the mass market in post-modern fashion culture
means that Newcastle provides, through its range of high-street outlets,
possibilities of fashionability for young women that are comparable to those
in London. Young women can reconstruct the latest magazine-inspired image
easily and cheaply in Newcastle. Although not in the vanguard of innovative
fashion, the city has in the past 20–30 years developed a lively identity of
fashion outlets, with many of the major national chains situated in the city
itself, or since 1986 in the nearby Metro Centre in Gateshead. The Eldon
Square centre is the major shopping concourse in Newcastle, and is situated
on the north side of the city. Fashion outlets directed at young women are
clustered in and around this area, and include French Connection, Oasis,
Top Shop, Miss Selfridge, Internacionale and latterly H&M. Major department
stores Fenwicks and John Lewis, as well as Marks & Spencer have outlets in
the Eldon Square complex, and Fenwicks contains a number of franchises,
including Kookai and Karen Millen. More exclusive fashion outlets are located
on the periphery of this area, although unlike Leeds, Glasgow or Manchester,
Newcastle lacks a strong base in the upper parts of the market. The expansion
of consumerism in the area through new shopping developments coincided
with the development of areas in the centre of Newcastle, such as the Quayside,
which offer an expanding culture of recreation for young people.

During the past ten years, a number of fashion outlets have developed
nationally that cater for a particular identity within the fourteen-to-twenty
age group. The look is post-Spice Girls in combining an infantilised and
overtly sexualised identity, and the first national outlet to have particular
success in its construction was Kookai. Following this company's success,
others such as Oasis, Warehouse and French Connection moved from catering
for a wider age group with a variety of looks to a more specific and mainstream image for a younger market. Other newer outlets, such as Jane
Norman, Pilot, Exhibit and New Look emerged at the end of the 1990s. The
clothes sold in these outlets are relatively cheap, many are overtly sexy
clothes 'to go out in'. There tends to be a strong colour theme identifiable
in all these retail sites. In 1999, both summer and winter clothes were
dominated by pink, mauve and black. These outfits would have been
described as party or special-occasion clothes 20 or 30 years ago, but are
now worn on any night of the week and often in daytime situations too.

Indeed, these are the kind of clothes that *Blue Peter* presenters now wear on children's TV. Revealing slinky tops and miniskirts with high heels, this image is a world away from Valerie Singleton's sensible shoes and modest dresses, and reflects the engagement of a younger age group with the apparatus of fashion and sexualised femininity.[26] These clothes put young women 'on show', spectacularising their appearance, often in situations in which this emphasis on their sexuality would seem to be irrelevant and inappropriate.

In Newcastle there are two major areas in the city itself where young people, and some older people 'go out'. There is the Bigg Market, a traditional drinking area where pubs have given way to bars but which is still characterised by a macho ambience. It is around the Bigg Market that most of the menswear outlets are positioned, and these sell designer clothes, although of a relatively unchallenging kind, as the overriding fashion identity for men is one of functionality. The Quayside is the other major area of recreation. This is an elegant stretch by the river in which older buildings and newly designed bars and cafes create an international feel. There has been enormous investment in this area, with post-modern law courts and award-winning architecture. The Quayside represents a feminised space, being light and spacious with a variety of restaurants, cafes and bars, in contrast to the more traditionally confined Bigg Market area. On Thursdays, Fridays and Saturdays the Quayside is thronged with young people famously having a good time.

Robert G. Hollands, in *Friday Night, Saturday Night*, an analysis of young people and recreation in Newcastle, writes, 'Two of the fundamental processes underlying changes in contemporary leisure and the phenomenon of going out are economic restructuring and the increasing role that the city plays in shaping young adults' experience of modern life'.[27] The clothes mentioned as a key element in contemporary fashion markets for young women are those fitted to the experience of going out at night in the city. There are other fashion and style identities for young people, but my interest here is in the image that dominates in this particular arena. These clothes are glamorous in nature, combining ostentation in terms of glossy and clingy materials with the erotic display of limbs and cleavage. It is in the last 10–15 years that this image has become noticeably more extreme as mainstream fashion has collapsed into the traditional tropes of glamorous clubwear.

In the mid-1980s the patterns of recreation that now dominate in the city could be first identified. Newcastle at night was full of allusions to Linda Evans and Joan Collins. Blonde perms or streaks, highly glamorous glittery clothes referred to the camp ostentation of *Dynasty*. Some of the notion of a stylised spectacular femininity, referred to in the first chapter and which connected with the first thrust of female commodification within capitalism, were to be found again in this period as Newcastle began to move from industrial centre to highly developed post-modern consumer culture. Thatcherism, with its emphasis on financial success and rejection of traditional working-class notions of community and identity, failed to destroy local community in recreational sites, but was represented by ostentation in fashion consumption. Dominant male style combined the ubiquitous Chris Waddle/Kevin Keegan back perm[28] with a fashion look influenced by Don Johnson in *Miami Vice*. By the late 1980s, the expansion of fashion retailing in the city for both sexes created a more sophisticated consumer market and the development of a more metropolitan fashion identity for young people. However, there is in the way that fashionable clothes are worn here by many a particular take on contemporary style that puts an emphasis on sexiness and strongly gendered bravura.

Going out in the city, even in the middle of winter, evokes summer nights in Ibiza or the Costa Brava. Every night is a party, an escapist adventure lived out on the streets and in the public spaces, and in contrast to the tedium of much female employment in the area and the persistence of dreary public housing. Hollands reports that 'Our research reveals that women go out more frequently, would feel worse if restricted and spend a higher percentage of their income on going out than their male counterparts'.[29] The 'girls night out' has become commonplace. It is no longer something that happens occasionally, or even just once a week. Young women go out together, enjoy each other's company, and may or may not 'pick up' a man. Interestingly, given the seductive nature of female dress, there is less emphasis on 'scoring' than there was 20–30 years ago, when girls danced round their handbags in dancehalls and clubs on a Saturday night, and the evening was a failure if no-one walked them home.

The fact that these young women are such avid consumers does not necessarily reflect their economic status in a city in which although there are more jobs for women than men, young men in work may be in higher-paid jobs. Twenty young women aged between sixteen and twenty-two were interviewed about their experience as fashion consumers in Newcastle in late 1998 and the beginning of 1999. The criteria used for the selection of this group was that they appeared to be interested in fashion and used the areas of the Bigg Market and Quayside regularly for recreation. Of the 20 in the sample, eight were in education, 12 in full-time employment. They were asked about their experience of fashion. In terms of their buying clothes, the group in education, of which three were still at school and the rest in further and higher education, spent more than those in employment. Seven of the eight students spent more than £50 a month on clothes, with one sixteen-year-old spending £200. Oasis was the most popular shop for this group, followed by Top Shop, Miss Selfridge, Jane Norman, Morgan and Internacionale. Oasis and Morgan are slightly more expensive than the other outlets in this sample, with an average outfit costing £35 to £40.

The employed group spent less as a rule, £30 as opposed to £50 a month, and for them Top Shop and Internacionale were the most popular outlets. The majority of these young women worked in service industries and were not well paid, as Hollands points out that in Newcastle 'many females are still limited to work in a narrow range of part time low paid serving jobs, characterised by poor promotion, a lack of training and low status'.[30]

The whole group used perfume and cosmetics. The most popular perfumes with most of those interviewed were Calvin Klein, Tommy Girl and Ralph Lauren, all of which have a high profile in the popular media and advertising campaigns that emphasise youthfulness as a characteristic of the consumer. Cosmetics in the majority of cases tended to be bought from cheaper ranges, such as Boots No 7, Rimmel and Avon. There was a sense of little real differentiation in the preferred look of most of these girls in a group that could be identified in traditional terms as working and lower-middle class. Those buying clothes from cheaper outlets were essentially committed to the same fashionable formula as those buying from Oasis or French Connection. Jennifer Craik, in *The Face of Fashion*, claims that 'at a general level, fashion is a technique of acculturation – a means by which individuals and groups learn to be visually at home with themselves in their culture'.[31]

There is a homogeneity about the female image. Elizabeth Wilson, in *The Sphinx in the City*, discusses the way in which the term post-modern can be used 'to suggest diversity and cultural variety but can also describe same-ness and emotional flatness'.[32] Whereas in previous decades status in terms of recreational sites might be defined by style and the exclusiveness of clothing as well as physical attractiveness, it is the body itself which would seem to be the principle signifier of value for young women in this context. It is in the past 10–15 years that this extreme polarisation of gendered identity has developed. At night on the Quayside, young women throng pubs like the Pitcher and Piano or the Chase Bar, hardly distinguishable one from another by their clothing or makeup. The Pitcher and Piano has been described as a 'girlie haunt'. It is an award-winning 'modernist' space with colour-washed walls, pine floors, open views across the Tyne. Quiet and sophisticated during the day, at night its character changes and it seethes with customers whose raucous behaviour is ostensibly at odds with the intended cool ambience of the setting. Tensions are created by this uneasy relationship between the post-modern restraint of the Quayside as a whole and the volatile nature of the young consumers who crowd the bars and cafes (Figure 5.2). The intended metropolitan sophistication of the area is subverted by the particular energy of these groups, which does not conform to the patterns of behaviour expected in such a 'Europeanised' arena and imposes its own dynamic on this stretch of ground. The river itself, historically associated with a different Newcastle, a city centred on shipbuilding and the export of

Figure 5.2: Girls drinking on the Quayside, Newcastle-upon-Tyne, December 1998. North News and Pictures, Newcastle-upon-Tyne.

coal, provides a dark counterpoint to the imposition of the cultural values of high capitalism along its banks.

The community created in these sites is one in which women are reduced to their corporeal selves. Traditionally it was the club or the dance hall in which young women paraded their sexuality. These were contained spaces in which for a short period rituals of attraction and courtship were enacted. Today both sexes in Newcastle famously go without coats in both winter and summer, and the contemporary nature of recreation and the fluidity of public space in areas such as the Quayside means that young women are 'on show' in a wider terrain (Figure 5.3). The highly gendered nature of fashion in this context sustains an inequality in relation to male and female display and sexuality. Women are spending more than men on recreation, and have effectively encroached on the spaces of masculinity, but the ubiquitous visibility of their bodies is at once a destabilising and yet reassuring factor in a city historically suffused with the culture of working-class masculinity. Elizabeth Wilson, in discussing the role of women in the city, states that 'the contemporary urban woman is both consumer and consumed...she remains an object of consumption at the same time as she becomes an actor'.[33]

The dominant look for young men in Newcastle consists of a shirt out over trousers or jeans, or a football top worn in the same way, ensuring that

Figure 5.3: Girls on the town. Newcastle-
upon-Tyne. North News and Pictures,
Newcastle-upon-Tyne.

the body is covered and disguised. Men may be spending more on clothes, more are going to the gym, but their bodies remain camouflaged by their clothing in the heterosexual arena. Evidence of the greater investment by men in the cosmetics industry is reflected in figures published by Colipa, the European cosmetics industry body, in June 1999, which suggested that an upturn in sales of male skin-care products and toiletries has resulted in the biggest growth in sales in the industry in the past ten years. Even in a city like Newcastle, which in many ways is still identified with traditional tropes of masculinity, there are high levels of consumption in these areas. Men are concerned with grooming and personal fitness, but their identity is overridingly attached to a traditional machismo.

There is a seeming confidence and assertiveness about the behaviour of the young women who parade through the city at night. In the heightened hedonistic atmosphere of Newcastle these young women are enjoying them-selves 'as if there is no tomorrow'. In a society in which relationships may be unstable and jobs often insecure, the future for many young women in the Northeast is particularly precarious, and the moment is lived with a greater celebratory intensity. Journalist Jeremy Clarke, in a recent article in the *Independent on Sunday*, 'Legless in Gazzaland', claiming to be an attempt to understand the cultural terrain of the footballer Paul Gascoigne, described a scene on the Quayside: 'I see hundreds of young women with next to nothing on roaming the streets in shrill gangs. Also I see a woman with hardly any clothes on withdrawing money from a cashpoint machine, while continuing her conversation with a man in drag who is urinating against the wall.'[34] An article in the *Guardian*, 'City Nights Out Never to be Remembered', although purporting to be concerned with the drinking culture of Newcastle, focused almost exclusively on the behaviour of young women in the city. 'Drink doesn't come cheap,' said one of the girls, 'it sets you back fifty pounds sometimes, although I can get through a whole lot more'. The photograph accompanying the piece was titled 'Party Girls'.[35]

The press and television frequently use Newcastle to illustrate the idea of a hedonistic, 'fun' city. Coverage may include images of girls, often drunk, standing outside pubs and bars. A Tyne Tees Television series called *Party Nights* recently featured a group of men from London who came to the Northeast regularly because of the alleged 'friendliness' of the women. 'They are not shy retiring-type girls. If it's sex you want it's sex you will get', commented one. A recent review in the *Independent on Sunday* of a book of photographs organised by the photographer's agency Magnum to observe the way in which the millennium was celebrated across Britain included images of Newcastle, one of which is of a girl in stretchy lycra pulling down her dress to expose her breasts.[36] It is an image that is more outrageous than those illustrated from other cities, and again emphasises the high visibility of a sexualised female identity and the identification of overt sexual display with women in the Northeast. In the adult comic *Viz*, the cartoon strip 'Fat Slags' has long ridiculed the notion of female empowerment in the traditionally masculine terrain of the city by a sexist portrayal of women who fail to conform to any rules concerning appropriately 'ladylike' behaviour and appearance. The spectacularisation of Newcastle itself in the media has positioned young women here as hedonistic and sexually abandoned, in a way more excessive and shocking than is the popular norm.

Interestingly, there is a seeming lack of inhibition about size amongst some young women in the city. Girls interviewed were very concerned with their bodies, and expressed anxieties about body shape but some who were larger than the desirable ideal wore the same revealing clothing as their slimmer peers. In the self-scrutinising culture of the 1960s, there were unspoken rules about who should wear the 'micro-skirt', and fat legs were to be disguised or covered but in Newcastle in 1999 the return of the micro-skirt, and the 'crop-top', was seemingly embraced by all, and this has to be seen on one level as a subversive element in what is predominantly a highly stereotypical scenario of female appearance.

Such minimal clothing as described is highly impractical in the pre-dominantly chill Newcastle nights, and at times appears to parody the images of fashion and femininity that dominate the popular media. Skirts are often that bit shorter, that bit tighter, than on the pages of *More* or *Just Seventeen*, cleavages that bit lower, hair that bit blonder and bigger, alluding to Pamela Anderson rather than Kate Moss. This stylisation could be read on one level as heterosexual camp, a hyper-femininity that carries a disorientating visual power and positions women centre-stage in the contemporary urban landscape. Such emphatically signalled femininity is tied to traditional working-class female identities, as represented by characters such as Bet Lynch in ITVs long-running soap *Coronation Street*. As glamour has become the mainstay of female fashion, and young women from all walks of life engage in 'babe culture', there has been a change in the significance of this identity in class terms, which it could be argued leads to even greater stylistic excess in sites such as Newcastle.

The relatively recent proliferation of soft pornography through satellite television, video and the internet could be seen as contributive to the style of self-presentation that we find here. The expansion of the Ann Summers empire, with its catalogues, parties and shops positioned in the centre of major towns, has helped to make the overtly erotic increasingly acceptable.[37] Elizabeth Wilson states, 'Clothing, in fact, has the unique characteristic of being able to express ideas about the body while simultaneously it actually adorns the body. Its ecstatic fantasy articulates sex on the body of the wearer'.[38] The clothes worn here are unequivocally sexual, they are at times minimal, almost to the point of irrelevance, and emphasise the binary opposition of male and female and the historical imperative of woman as sex.

Young men in Newcastle sport designer labels alongside the football shirts, and there is a sense in which fashion for them is concerned with peer-group status. For women, the quality and identity of clothes themselves seems less important than the way in which they expose and foreground the body. The excessive emphasis on sexuality in this site could be read as a mask in which femininity is inscribed with particular local anxieties about the status of masculinity in a city in which traditional industry has been decimated. There is something at times brutally confrontational about the dominant 'Geordie' masculine identity characterised by fanatical support for Newcastle United Football Club in a culture still centred around heavy drinking. Although such an identity is common in other northern industrial cities, the geographical remoteness and intermittent cultural marginality of Newcastle contributes to a sense that it is a 'frontier town', a place characterised at night by excess and lack of inhibition. The city is unique in the context of other major English cities in that although there are Asian and Chinese communities there is a very small Afro-Caribbean one, and the city therefore lacks the dimension of difference and the particular cultural energy that such communities have brought to other urban centres. Years of economic insecurity and deprivation in the twentieth century have contributed to 'a live now pay later' ethos in which there is a sense of edgy desperation as well as enjoyment.

Fashion in general in the past decade and longer has been consistent in referring to the 1950s and 1960s, but the 1960s have been the strongest influence, and this can be seen in the type of clothes that I have described as being worn by young women at night in Newcastle. Shift or slip dresses, miniskirts or straight skirts all refer to fashion lines from that period. The fact that this engagement with the 1960s has been a constant element in fashion is interesting on a number of levels. The expansion of consumerism, social change and new youth markets in the 1960s helped to create a cultural charge that was represented in style and fashion by a sharp definitive take on modernity. It seems that the style of high modernity has come to represent what it is to be young and contemporary. Fashionable imagery of that period is associated with fun and excitement, but also offers the contemporary consumer the security of an 'absolute stylishness'. Those grainy videos of *Ready Steady Go* present us with images of consummate cool. The restraint of the modern, the less is more chic of Mary Quant or John Bates represent an aesthetic for the young that has been identified as quintessentially twentieth century. Charles Jencks claimed a symbolic significance in architecture for the transition from modernism to post-modernism in the deliberate destruction of the Pruitt-Igoe Building in St Louis, Missouri in 1972;[39] in fashion such a moment can be identified in the studied eclecticism of Biba in Britain in the later 1960s. From that point, the pursuit of originality and inventiveness that had reached its zenith in designs of Courreges and John Bates in the mid-1960s surfaced only briefly and intermittently, and were overwhelmed by a relentless trawling of the past in the ever-expanding fashion industry.

The mid-1960s was also – and this is of particular significance in relation to contemporary female imagery – a period of greater clarity in relation to gendered roles and identity, while fashion itself took on larger cultural significance as markets broadened and the process became at once more democratic and more sophisticated. The female fashion image of the mid-1960s was one of the most problematic of the twentieth century, at once infantilised and sexualised. 'The Look', as it was called, operated around a highly fetishised identity played across by tensions relating to new developments in contraception and a newly emphatic female presence in the public arena.

The process by which the sexual had been separated from the reproductive in dominant female imagery in the modern period was accentuated in the 1960s by an emphasis on extreme slimness. The image referred to a sexualised identity, but with its stress on thinness and stylised child-like qualities it represents a highly fraught model in relation to issues of power and identity.

The allusions to the pre-adult female, and associations with the fun of youth as a counterpoint to the responsibilities of adulthood is something we find in the emphasis on 'girliness' in contemporary fashion and iconography with its succession of 'babes'. It was in the 1960s that there was a re-emphasis on the imperative of youth as an ideal for femininity, a feature that Jennifer Craik identified as initially emerging in markets in the 1920s: 'The Image of "The Girl" [as opposed to the Woman] became synonymous with the exchange of value attached to consumer goods, "the coin in the exchange of desire"'.[40] In the later 1950s, teenage markets were instrumental in the construction of images of youthful femininity, and this was taken into the 1960s and refined as something highly stylised, and in many ways problematic.

From 1963, emphasis on the techniques of femininity moved up a gear and the expanding fashion media stressed the value of femininity as spectacle. This increase in objectification coincided with the rumblings of feminism. What significance does the reiteration of these stylistic mores have for young women in contemporary cultures? Fashion is not fixed, but fluid; meanings change, and in post-modern culture different eclectic elements are combined to affect nuance, but nevertheless it is hard to deny that our preoccupation with this period has a particular significance for women. Are these contemporary images suffused with irony, has the meaning of these clothes radically altered in the hands of a more knowing and emancipated generation, or do they still carry with them references to unresolved tensions in relation to female status and sexuality?

It was the reworking of this 1960s identity that collapsed into the notion of 'girl power', ever crystallised in the image of Geri Halliwell wearing her union-jack mini-dress. It would perhaps be simplistic to argue that in Susan Faludi's terms this re-emergence of the infantilised female type in the 1990s represents a form of backlash against female success in a changing society and culture. It is certainly ironic that at a moment when many girls are surpassing boys in academic achievement, and we see an increasing feminisation of work cultures, the prevalent images for women are of a girlie playfulness. Allusions to the substance of women's lives are lost in a sea of pink and flowery embroidery. Fashion and beauty markets operate around the elusive, and in a culture in which the areas of plastic surgery and youth-sustaining cosmetics are ever more successful and expanding, the construction of a fashion identity that connects to the pert attributes of the young teenager also feeds the anxieties of the affluent and ageing 'baby-boomer' generation.

In terms of the younger generation, statistics on sexual health[41] and teenage pregnancies in Britain are a telling subtext to the media promotion of sexually assertive 'babes' and the seeming confidence with which young women on Tyneside conduct themselves. The Northeast of England has the worst record in Britain for teenage pregnancies and sexually transmitted diseases. In an article published in the *Guardian* in July 1996, Beatrix Campbell interviewed a group of young women about their nights out and found an interesting variety of responses and experiences.[42] The pleasures and new freedoms attached to a culture in which women have gained access to new recreational spaces were weighed against the continuing anxieties and dissatisfactions in relation to men. Poverty and low educational expectation are underlying factors in the difficulties that exist in relation to sexual experience for many young women in the region, and I am interested in the significance of the increasing sexualisation of dress in this context. A promotion of a highly stereotypical eroticised appearance as an indicator of female sexual power has a different significance in a sophisticated and affluent metropolitan arena (although I would still question its value as empowering in this context) from that which it carries in other sites in which women's equality has not been supported by financial empowerment and educational opportunity, and where such an overt emphasis on woman as body could be said to reinforce historical stereotypes.

Angela McRobbie claims that

femininity is no longer the 'other' of feminism; instead it incorporates many of those structures of feeling which emerged from the political discourse of feminism in the 1970s. But it also and perhaps most powerfully exists as a product of a highly charged consumer culture which in turn provides subject positions for girls and personal identities for them through consumption.[43]

It is in the tensions that result from this relationship between established ideology and the market that create what is often a conflicted and difficult position for young women in a consumer culture that reduces all sexual experience to fun and ignores the continuing complexities that exist for women in relation to sexuality, and the relationship between sexuality and reproduction. The type of female iconography that dominates the popular media as consumed by these young women is inextricably tied to fashion and the concept of girl power already mentioned.

When asked about the notion of girl power, the group of young women interviewed gave varied responses. One girl, a seventeen-year-old student, said that it was 'Great, but some girls take it too far', considering them too 'loud and pushy'. A number thought it was rubbish. Those who agreed with it seemed to consider it a new development of 'women's lib.', although none seemed to take it very seriously. Their role models, however, did seem to represent that combination of media glamour and girlishness associated with the term and its original association with the Spice Girls. Denise Van Outen was the most popular choice of role model for the group, with Kate Moss and Martine McCutcheon following in her wake. There was no mention of film stars or other figures whose significance lay outside the fashion/music/popular-television-celebrity axis.

Denise Van Outen is in some ways a disturbing role model. A product of stage school, she became best known for her role as Johnny Vaughan's wise-cracking sidekick on *The Big Breakfast* on Channel Four. Her professional relationship with Vaughan with whom she engaged in an ironically pitched and at times witty dialogue on The Big Breakfast, marked her out as a 'laddette' and icon for the men's magazines *Loaded* and *FHM*. She combined being impossibly sexy at seven o' clock in the morning with a matey sense of humour and 'good' personality, although not good enough to threaten Johnny Vaughan's pivotal role as the main presenter of the programme. Her image combined infantilisation with knowing sexiness. She wore schoolgirl bunches in her hair, little 'girlie' outfits that revealed a toned and tanned body. She had obviously spent longer in 'makeup' in the early hours of the morning than the louche Johnny Vaughan, whose casual and low-key appearance added to a sense of effortlessness and superiority in his style of presentation. Her persona was identified with fun, and not taking herself or life too seriously.

Angela McRobbie, in *Post-modernism and Popular Culture*, refers to the fact that 'there is a greater uncertainty in Society as a whole about what it is to be a woman and this filters down to how young women exist within this new habitus of gender relations'.[44] On the surface, young women are presented with fashions and associated commodities that are identified as fun. Pinks and pale blues, glittery tops, childish hair slides, bunches represent fashion and femininity as a playground, where adult women can revert to living in the kitsch ambience of a 'Barbie world'. After years of women being margin-alised within recreational cultures and contained by notions of duty and propriety, the idea of being part of a pleasure-orientated milieu dominated by the superficial and transient is seductive. The image of a Van Outen, who seemingly meets the alleged desires of contemporary men in combining a drinking mate with sex object who does not 'get too heavy' or become too serious, represents a post-Thatcherite role model for young women, in combining conventional female sexiness with financial success. This model has succeeded the more puritanical work-orientated goals of an older generation of women. It is not surprising, therefore, that interviews with young women in Newcastle found that across class the most popular magazine amongst the group was *More*, a publication that both promulgates and celebrates these values.

Angela McRobbie, in her book *In the Culture Society*, chooses to discuss the status of *More* within the contemporary magazine economy in relation to the construction of new sexualities.[45] *More* is published every two weeks. It is much preoccupied with sex, and particularly it seems with sexual technique. McRobbie identifies it as having an ironic tone, and this is the case of earlier copies of the magazine, in which the irony is relentless and the editorial approach jokey. A copy from December 1998 flagged up features entitled 'Twigs up your bum: the joys of sex outdoors', 'Get bigger boobs: how to top up what's on top'. By October 1999, there were articles titled 'Look good naked: get your kit off with confidence' and 'Peachy: cheat your away to the perfect bum'. These continue the theme of sexy cosmetic tips, but there is a sense in which the tone has become less ironic. As McRobbie points out, the magazine is read by an age group starting from the early teens and reaching up to the mid-twenties. The fashion is high street, with articles on pub fashion operating alongside features concerned essentially with familiar celebrities such as Denise Van Outen and Geri Halliwell. The first edition of *More* of 2000 contained the obligatory pictures of Zoë Ball and Denise Van Outen in the gossip section. A fashion feature, 'Dusk till dawn', promoted the usual minimalist glamour and the 'look of the fortnight' was entitled 'Bad girls rock on in high heels and trashy tops'. A section at the back of the magazine describes incidents where sex-play ended in a trip to a hospital casualty department, and the sexual position of the fortnight is the 'love kneel'!

As with the generalised look of most of the young women on the Quayside, there is little room in these magazines for difference. The models are predominantly white, blonde, size ten, with a ubiquitous predilection for pink. *More* sometimes features black male pin-ups, but there are few images of black women. The clothes that are promoted come predominantly from familiar high-street outlets such as French Connection, Warehouse, New Look, Jane Norman, River Island and Top Shop, sources accessible to the majority of readers (Figure 5.4). With the October 1999 copy of the magazine, there came a separate guide on 'Good sex', including sections on 'What he's thinking about when you're doing it' and 'Mind blowing! Oral sex tips from Blokes'. The culture of romance that dominated young women's traditional popular reading materials, as discussed by Angela McRobbie in her work on *Jackie* magazine[46] has now been superseded by a preoccupation with relationships with men based on sex. The emphasis is still on relationships with men, and there are few if any articles about interests outside these relationships. These preoccupations are represented in the type of fashion imagery and advertising that accompany the editorial. The notion that the representation of female sexuality in contemporary culture is suffused with irony, and that this supposed irony somehow ameliorates the obsessive cultural preoccupations with surface appearance and sexual performance, seems dubious. There is a line between fun and trivialisation, and a magazine like *More* and many of the fashions that it promotes cross that line. The culture of such magazines is one that clearly rejects the feminism of an older generation.

Looking at copies of *Honey* from the early 1980s, aimed at an equivalent market in age, one is struck immediately by a difference in tone. There were articles about improving the female body by exercise and cosmetics, but there were also articles about changing jobs and a series in which women wrote about their greatest female influences. There is a section on 'Losers in love', and there are discussions about sex, but the subject does not dominate the text. Fashion plays a significant part in the magazine, but there do seem to be a wider range of stylistic identities available than in the contemporary fashion media. *Honey*, from its instigation in the 1960s, offered a broader choice of options for women than is the case with a magazine such as *More*. Obviously, given the nature of the period, the content of *Honey* was rife with tensions and contradictions, but options for young women as offered in contemporary magazines such as *More* seem to have been reduced to a superficial engagement with the popular media and an overwhelming emphasis on sex and how to be 'sexy'.

The success of *More*, *Shine* and a revitalised *Nineteen* have affected the sales of more expensive and upmarket fashion-oriented magazines such as

Figure 5.4: The window display in Top Shop, Eldon Square,
Newcastle-upon-Tyne, December 1998.

Elle. In an article in the *Guardian*, published in May 1999, the editor of *Elle*, Fiona McIntosh, described her approach to falling sales figures through a 'return to feminine values and a colour palette of mints and lilacs and pinks and sky blues'.[47] In June, she presented the 'Sex 2000 issue' featuring the ubiquitous Denise Van Outen and her partner Jay Kay on the cover. The stylish restraint of the old *Elle*, with its metropolitan design values and relatively articulate factual articles, has given way to a more 'fun' approach, privileging sex over style.

A study of sexuality amongst young people over the ten years between 1988 and 1998, 'The Male in the Head', adds further unsurprising if depressing evidence to support the fact that the experience of the majority of women, and in this case young women, is not in reality the fun-filled 'Barbie world' that fashion and the popular media would seem to suggest. The world of sex and glamour represented in contemporary fashion for young women, which implies a sophisticated sexual identity, belies a reality in which heterosexuality is still fraught with anxieties and misunderstandings. The authors report that many of the young women interviewed for the purposes of the book 'suggest that they are under pressure to construct their bodies into a model of femininity which is both inscribed on the surface through such skills as dress, makeup and dietary regimes, and disembodied, in the sense of detachment from their sensuality and alienation from their material bodies',[48] and that 'In their sexual relationships they were still largely dependent on the way the men that they were with defined the sexual encounter'.[49]

Elaine Knox, discussing the status of women in Newcastle in a book published in 1992, claimed that

> Tyneside's women have achieved through work an economic and social revolution without waging cultural war. Sid the Sexist may roam between the Tuxedo Royale and Bentleys, but the Fat Slags have beaten him at his own game. Confident, working and with money to spend and leisure time earned, they have taken elements of that masculine work-based heritage – the noisy assertion of the right to enjoy life, to spend hard earned money on hedonistic pursuits and the belief in the importance of their region and its identity – and made them their own.[50]

This is a highly optimistic account of the cultural and economic power of young women in the Northeast of England, emphasising areas of pleasure and recreation. It disregards the dislocation between image and experience, the public and the private in which fashion plays a key role. Fashion is not just a superficial, fun aspect of women's lives, it is part of the culture that shapes our experience. The gulf between the reality of women's lives, which is ever more complex, and the one-dimensional images of women promoted through the fashion system has never been more striking. The identification of young women on Tyneside with the world of drunken abandon, once the terrain of men, does not signify greater empowerment. The traditional 'colliers Saturday night', during which the rigours and difficulties of life could be erased in drinking to excess has now come to represent the principal identity of both sexes in the de-industrialised city. There is fun to be had in the Quayside and Bigg Market, but many of the young women there have lives as workers as mothers, often difficult and fragmented lives. These social realities are rendered invisible in the fantasy of constant carnival by which Newcastle is represented, just as the reality of young women's lives in general is distorted in the climate of contemporary fashion.

Popular feminism, which had such an impact on these issues 30 years ago, has largely failed to address them in the later part of the twentieth century. Naomi Wolf and Susan Faludi, whose work in the early 1990s was seen as a new onslaught on the position and representation of women within high capitalism, have been followed latterly by revisionist texts in which authors accommodate some of the post-feminist attitudes of the last five years. Natasha Walter's book *The New Feminism* was published in the late 1990s, and was an attempt to redefine feminism for her generation. Responsive to fashionable concerns about the position of men in an increasingly feminised society, she looks to a more consultative and conciliatory version of sexual politics than that supported by her mother's generation. She argues against women being divested of the pleasures of the fashion system:

> But women run health clubs and glossy magazines, cosmetic and fashion businesses. If the pressure to be beautiful was merely a male conspiracy, it would have run out of steam long ago. When I think back over a lifetime of contact with beauty culture…dressing up with my sister to go to teenage parties, carefully and lovingly doing each other's eyeliner and hair; or visiting salons where women young and old, white and black, preen in front of mirrors and engage their hairdressers or manicurists in fascinated conversation; or indeed working at a glossy magazine, where the hothouse, obsessive atmosphere produced complex cultural readings of a single pair of shoes – I adore the funny, female, comfortable atmosphere that rises back at me. An atmosphere that cossets the body, certainly, but doesn't degrade women or imprison them.[51]

Walter describes her personal experience of 'dipping into' the fashion and beauty culture with a lack of critical awareness and ignorance of the sophistication that characterises much academic feminist analysis of these issues. It is possible to accept the dimension of pleasure to be found for women in fashion whilst acknowledging the complex issues that lie at the heart of the positioning of women within it. Germaine Greer, who first alerted me to this subject long ago, produced her book *The Whole Woman* in 1999. The book was met by vociferous antagonism from some younger feminists, who believed that debates had moved on and Greer had not. Greer, whilst acknowledging the many positive changes in women's lives in the 30 years since *The Female Eunuch*, also deplores the escalation of a culture of beauty and fashion that takes its lead from the plastic unreality of Barbie and which now, through globalisation, is insinuating itself into cultures outside the West, in which women have little social or economic power and whose previous experience of femininity was shaped by different cultural values from our own: 'After the implosion of the USSR the first western shops to open in the old Soviet cities were cosmetic franchises; before a Russian woman could buy an orange or a banana she could buy a lipstick by Dior or Revlon'.[52]

There is within contemporary academic feminism a growing acknowledgement of our failure to address the problems that have arisen for women in the escalation of capitalism and consumer culture. Lynne Segal's book *Why Feminism?* builds on her impressive engagement with issues of gender and attempts to evaluate feminism in all its diversity at the end of the twentieth century. In her conclusion, she states that 'The special legacy of feminism lies in its striving to keep relating the personal and the cultural to the economic and the cultural however forbidding that enterprise may be'.[53] In our study of fashion, those relationships are central to a critique that is to be both theoretically trenchant and culturally influential. For young women to experience themselves as unified subjects there needs to be an ongoing and creative dialogue by feminists across generations to engage with the continuing problems that exist for women within the politics of appearance.

NOTES ON CHAPTER 5

1   *Honey*, magazine for young women first published in 1963.
2   Popular music programme on BBC television in the 1960s.
3   Germaine Greer, *The Female Eunuch* (London, Paladin, 1971), p.261.
4   Lisa Tickner, *Spare Rib*, 51, October 1976.
5   Laura Mulvey, *Spare Rib*, 8, February 1973.
6   Calvin Klein, 'The Great American Look', *Vogue*, March 1979, p.154.
7   Sonia Rykiel, Chloe, Christian Dior, *Vogue*, January 1976, pp.74–6.
8   *Vogue*, February 1976, pp.80–1, 106.
9   Caroline Evans and Minna Thornton, *Women and Fashion: A New Look* (London, Quartet, 1989), p.23.
10   Ibid., p.30.
11   Judith Williamson, *Decoding Advertisements* (London, Marion Boyars, 1978).
12   Rosalind Coward, *Female Desire* (London, Paladin, 1983).
13   Jane Root, *Pictures of Women: Sexuality* (London, Pandora, 1983).

14   Janice Winship, *Inside Women's Magazines* (London, Pandora, 1987).

15   Evans and Thornton, *Women and Fashion*, p.15.

16   Cathy Schwichtenberg (ed.), *The Madonna Connection: Representional Politics, Subcultural Identities and Cultural Theory* (Oxford, Westview Press, 1993), pp.167–87.

17   Naomi Wolf, *The Beauty Myth: How Images of Beauty are Used Against Women* (London, Chatto and Windus, 1990).

18   Susan Faludi, *Backlash: The Undeclared War Against Women* (London, Chatto and Windus, 1991)

19   Alexandra Warwick and Dani Cavallaro (eds), *Fashioning the Frame: Boundaries, Dress and the Body* (Oxford, Berg, 1998), p.14.

20   Schwichtenberg (ed.), *The Madonna Connection*, p.28.

21   Angela McRobbie, *Post-modernism and Popular Culture* (London, Routledge, 1994), p.129

22   Schwichtenberg (ed.), *The Madonna Connection*, p.181.

23   Ibid., p.161.

24   Ibid., p.269.

25   Steven Connor, *Postmodernist Culture: An Introduction to Theories of the Contemporary* (Oxford, Blackwell, 1989).

26   Valerie Singleton, presenter of *Blue Peter*, a BBC TV programme which has run since the 1960s.

27   Robert G. Hollands, *Friday Night, Saturday Night: Youth Cultural Identification in the Post-industrial City* (Department of Social Policy, University of Newcastle, Newcastle-upon-Tyne, 1995), p.12

28   Kevin Keegan and Chris Waddle played football for Newcastle United in the 1970s, and were famous not only for their footballing skills but also for their permed version of the mullet haircut.

29   Hollands, *Friday Night, Saturday Night*, p.21.

30   Ibid., p.13.

31   Jennifer Craik, *The Face of Fashion: Cultural Studies in Fashion* (London, Routledge, 1994), p.10.

32   Elizabeth Wilson, *The Sphinx in the City* (London, Virago, 1991), p.135.

33   Wilson, *The Sphinx in the City*, p.139.

34   Jeremy Clarke, 'Legless in Gazzaland', *Independent on Sunday*, 18 October 1998.

35   *Guardian*, 22 May 2000.

36   *Independent on Sunday*, 'Review', 23 January 2000, photograph by Bruce Gilden.

37   Ann Summers is a British firm selling erotica in stores and by party plan.

38   Juliet Ash and Elizabeth Wilson (eds), *Chic Thrills: A Fashion Reader* (London, Pandora, 1992), p.12.

39   Charles Jencks, *The Language of Post Modern Architecture* (London, Academy Editions, 1984), p.9.

40   Craik, *The Face of Fashion*, p.71.

41 *Guardian*, 14 May 1999, report on the *British Medical Journal* claim that Britain has the worst record for teenage pregnancy, sexual disease and abortion in Europe.

42 Beatrix Campbell, 'Girls on Safari', *Guardian*, 15 June 1996.

43 McRobbie, *Post-modernism and Popular Culture*, p.173.

44 Ibid., p.157.

45 Angela McRobbie, *In the Culture Society: Art, Fashion and Popular Music* (London, Routledge, 1999), Ch. 4.

46 Angela McRobbie, *Feminism and Youth Culture: Jackie to Just Seventeen* (London, Macmillan, 1991), p.81.

47 Hette Judah, 'Pulling the Girls', *Guardian*, 17 May 1999.

48 Janet Holland, Caroline Ramazanoglu, Sue Sharpe and Rachel Thomson (eds), *The Male in the Head: Young People, Heterosexuality and Power* (London, The Tuffnell Press, 1998), p.111.

49 Ibid., p.113.

50 Robert Colls and Bill Lancaster (eds), *Geordies* (Edinburgh, Edinburgh University Press, 1992), p.112.

51 Natasha Walter, *The New Feminism* (London, Virago, 1999), p.88.

52 Germaine Greer, *The Whole Woman* (London, Doubleday, 1999), p.26.

53 Lynn Segal, *Why Feminism? Gender, Psychology and Politics* (Cambridge, Polity Press, 1999), p.231.

Select Bibliography

Addressing the Century: 100 Years of Art and Fashion (London, Hayward Gallery, 1998)

Alexander, Sally, *Becoming a Woman and Other essays in 19th and 20th Century Feminist History* (London, Virago, 1994)

Ash, Juliet and Elizabeth Wilson (eds), *Chic Thrills: A Fashion Reader* (London, Pandora, 1992)

Ballaster, Ros et al. (eds), *Women's Worlds: Ideology, Femininity and the Gail Woman's Magazine* (London, Macmillan, 1991)

Barker, Pat, *Regeneration* (London, Viking, 1991)

Beckett, Jane and Deborah Cherry, *The Edwardian Era* (London, Phaidon Press, 1987)

Beddoe, Deirdre, *Back to Home and Duty: Women Between the Wars, 1918–1939* (London, Pandora, 1989)

Beetham, Margaret, *A Magazine of Her Own: Domesticity and Desire in the Woman's Magazine, 1800–1914* (London, Routledge, 1996)

Benson, Susan P., *Counter Cultures: Saleswomen, Managers and Customers in American Department Stores, 1890–1940* (Urbana and Chicago, University of Illinois Press, 1988)

Betterton, Rosemary, *An Intimate Distance: Women, Artists and the Body* (Routledge, London, 1996)

Braidotti, Rosi, *Nomadic Subjects: Embodiment and Sexual Difference in Contemporary Feminist Theory* (New York, Columbia University Press, 1994)

Braybon, Gail and Penny Summerfield, *Out of the Cage: Women's Experiences in Two World Wars* (London, Pandora, 1987)

Breward, Christopher, *The Culture of Fashion: A New History of Fashionable Dress* (Manchester, Manchester University Press, 1995)

Brown, Denise, S. and Robert Venturi, *Complexity and Contradiction in Architecture* (New York, Museum of Modern Art, 1966)

Brown, Denise, S. and Robert Venturi, *Learning From Las Vegas* (London, MIT Press, 1972)

Burman, Barbara, *The Culture of Sewing: Gender, Consumption and Home Dressmaking* (Oxford, Berg, 1999)

Butler, Judith, *Gender Trouble: Feminism and the Subversion of Identity* (London, Routledge, 1990)

Collis, Robert and Bill Lancaster (eds), *Geordies* (Edinburgh University Press, 1992)

Craik, Jennifer, *The Face of Fashion: Cultural Studies in Fashion* (London, Routledge, 1994)

Drake, Barbara, *Women in Trade Unions* (London, Virago, 1984)

Dyer, Richard, *White* (London, Routledge, 1997)

Evans, Caroline and Minna Thornton, *Women and Fashion: A New Look* (London, Quartet Books, 1989)

Ewing, Elizabeth, *History of 20th Century Fashion* (London, Batsford, 1992)

Faulkner, Thomas, E., *Northumbrian Panorama: Studies in the History and Culture of North East England* (London, Octavian Press, 1996)

Ferguson, Marjorie, *Forever Feminine: Women's Magazines and the Cult of Femininity* (London, Heinemann, 1983)

Garber, Marjorie, *Vested Interests: Cross Dressing and Cultural Anxiety* (Penguin, London, 1993)

Gilroy, Paul, *The Black Atlantic Modernity and Double Consciousness* (London, Verso, 1993)

Gittins, Diana, *Fair Sex: Family Size and Structure 1900–1939* (London, Hutchinson, 1982)

Gledhill, Christine, *Stardom: Industry of Desire* (London, Routledge, 1991)

Hall, Radclyffe, *The Well of Loneliness* (London, Cape, 1928)

Hardyment, Christina, *From Mangle to Microwave: The Mechanisation of Household Work* (London, Polity Press, 1988)

Haste, Cate, *Rules of Desire: Sex in Britain, World War 1 to the Present* (London, Chatto and Windus, 1992)

Heron, Liz, *Truth, Dare or Promise: Girls Growing Up in the 50s* (London, Virago, 1985)

Higonnet, Margaret R. and Jane Jenson (eds), *Behind the Lines: Gender and the Two World Wars* (New York, Yale University Press, 1987)

Hobsbawn, Eric, *The Age of Extremes: The Short Twentieth Century 1914-1991* (London, Michael Joseph, 1994)

Hollands, Robert G., *Friday Night, Saturday Night: Youth Cultural Identification in the Post-industrial City* (Newcastle-upon-Tyne, The Department of Social Policy, University of Newcastle-upon-Tyne, 1995)

Holtby, Winifred, *Women and a Changing Civilisation* (London, John Lane, 1934)

hooks, bell, *Yearning: Race, Gender and Cultural Politics* (London, Turnaround, 1991)

Jefferys, James B., *Retail Trading in Britain 1850–1950* (Cambridge, Cambridge University Press, 1954)

Jephcott, A. Pearl, *Girls Growing Up* (London, Faber and Faber, 1942)

Jones, Gareth, *Workers at Play: A Social and Economic History of Leisure 1918–1939* (London, Routledge & Kegan Paul, 1986)

Kent, Susan Kingsley, *Making Peace: The Reconstruction of Gender in Interwar Britain* (Princeton, Princeton University Press, 1993)

Kuhn, Annette, *Women's Pictures: Feminism and Cinema* (London, Routledge, 1982)

Lancaster, William, *The History of the Department Store* (Leicester, Leicester University Press, 1995)

Light, Alison, *Forever England: Femininity, Literature and Conservatism Between the Wars* (London, Routledge, 1991)

Mackerell, Alice, *Paul Poiret* (London, Batsford, 1990)

Marwick, Arthur, *Women at War 1914–1918* (London, Fontana, 1977)

Massey, Doreen, *Space, Place, Gender* (Cambridge, Polity Press, 1994)

Mattelart, Michele, *Women Media Crisis: Femininity and Disorder* (London, Comedia, 1986)

McCraken, Ellen, *Decoding Women's Magazines* (Basingstoke, Macmillan, 1993)

McDowell, Colin, *Directory of Twentieth Century Fashion* (London, Muller, 1974)

McRobbie, Angela, *Zoot Suits and Second-Hand Dresses: An Anthology of Fashion and Music* (London, Macmillan, 1989)

McRobbie, Angela, *Post-modernism and Popular Culture* (Routledge, London, 1994)

McRobbie, Angela, *British Fashion Design: Rag Trade or Image Industry?* (London, Routledge, 1998)

Mordaunt Crook, J., *The Rise and Fall of the Nouveaux Riches* (John Murray, London, 1999)

Moss, Michael and Alison Turton, *A Legend of Retailing...House of Fraser* (London, Weidenfield & Nicholson, 1989)

Mowat, Charles L., *Britain Between the Wars 1918–1940* (Cambridge, Methuen, 1987)

Nava, Mica, and Alan O'Shea, *Modern Times Reflections on a Century of English Modernity* (London, Routledge, 1996)

Orr, Clarissa C., *Women in the Victorian Art World* (Manchester, Manchester University Press, 1995)

Orwell, George, *Coming Up for Air* (London, Penguin, 1990, first published 1939)

Orwell, George, 'England Your England', in *Inside the Whale and Other Essays* (London, Penguin, 2001)

Poiret, Paul, *My First Fifty Years* (London, Gollancz, 1934)

Pollock, Griselda, *Differencing the Canon: Feminist Desire and the Writings of Art's Histories* (London, Routledge, 1999)

Priestley, J.B., *The Edwardians* (Heinemann, London, 1970)

Pugh, Martin, *Women and The Women's Movement in Britain 1914–1959* (London, Macmillan, 1992)

Rappaport, Erika, *Diane Shopping for Pleasure: Women in the Making of London's West End* (Princeton University Press, 2000)

Reed, Christopher, *Not at Home: The Suppression of Domesticity in Modern Art and Architecture* (London, Thames and Hudson, 1996)

Rees, Goronwy, *St Michael: A History of Marks & Spencer* (London, Weidenfeld and Nicholson, 1969)

Reeves, Maud P., *Round About A Pound A Week* (London, Virago, 1994)

Rice, Margery S., *Working-class Wives* (London, Virago, 1981)

Richards, Jeffrey, *The Age of the Dream Palace: Cinema and Society in Britain 1930–1939* (London, Routledge & Kegan Paul, 1984)

Rowbotham, Sheila, *A New World For Women: Stella Browne – Socialist Feminist* (London, Pluto Press, 1978)

Rowbotham, Sheila, *Hidden From History* (London, Pluto Press, 1973)

Schwichtenberg, Cathy (ed.), *The Madonna Connection: Representational Politics, Subcultural Identities and Cultural Theory* (Westview Press, Oxford, 1993)

Segal, Lynne, *Why Feminism? Gender, Psychology and Politics* (Polity Press, London, 1999)

Showalter, Elaine, *Sexual Anarchy: Gender and Culture at the Fin de Siècle* (London, Bloomsbury, 1991)

Smith, Alison, *The Victorian Nude: Sexuality, Morality and Art* (Manchester, Manchester University Press, 1996)

Stacey, Jackie, *Star Gazing: Hollywood Cinema and Female Spectatorship* (London, Routledge, 1994)

Steele, Valerie, *Fashion and Eroticism: Ideals of Feminine Beauty from the Victorian to the Jazz Age* (Oxford, Oxford University Press, 1985)

Stevenson, John, *British Society 1914–45* (London, Pelican, 1984)

Stopes, Marie, *Married Love* (A.C. Fifield, 1918)

Taylor, Lou, and Elizabeth Wilson, *Through the Looking Glass: A History of Dress from 1860 to the Present Day* (London, BBC, 1989)

Tickner, Lisa, *The Spectacle of Women: Imagery of the Suffrage Campaign 1907–14* (London, Chatto & Windus, 1987)

Ware, Vron, *Beyond the Pale: White Women, Racism and History* (London, Verso, 1992)

White, Cynthia, *Women's Magazines, 1693–1968* (London, Michael Joseph, 1970)

Williams, Gertrude, *The New Democracy: Women and Work* (London, Nicholson & Watson, 1945)

Wilson, Elizabeth, *Adorned in Dreams: Fashion and Modernity* (London, Virago, 1985)

Wilson, Elizabeth, *The Sphinx in the City* (Virago, London, 1991)

Winship, Janice, *Inside Women's Magazines* (London, Pandora Press, 1987)

Index